RISING
ABOVE AND BEYOND
THE
CROSSBAR

RISING

ABOVE AND BEYOND
THE
CROSSBAR

THE LIFE STORY OF LINCOLN "TIGER" PHILLIPS

Lincoln A. Phillips

As told to Robert Clarke
With research by Valentino Singh

authorHOUSE®

AuthorHouse™ LLC
1663 Liberty Drive
Bloomington, IN 47403
www.authorhouse.com
Phone: 1-800-839-8640

Published by AuthorHouse   03/26/2014

ISBN: 978-1-4918-6248-3 (sc)
ISBN: 978-1-4918-6249-0 (e)

Library of Congress Control Number: 2014902404

Contents

Foreword

In today's footballing world—of global television rights, highly paid megastars, and the mad scramble to get a larger slice of a shrinking pie—it is easy to forget what this game really means, where it has come from, and what it should ultimately stand for.

It is even easier to forget what motivated the pioneers of football. How many times did they pick themselves up, dust themselves off, and soldier on in pursuit of a future that was as unclear to them then as the past can be to us now?

Let me be frank: I heard about Lincoln Phillips long before I had the fortune of meeting or working with him. He went to school with my father, and played in goal for Trinidad and Tobago. His feats in both places provided the first chapters of the legend that is his life. His career as soccer coach of Howard University, the college I also attended and played for, furnished the chapters that follow.

As my own career developed, even I couldn't deny the parallels between us. I seemed to be following a path blazed by a man who has been roundly and rightly praised for the direction he set.

Growing up and playing football in Trinidad and Tobago arms you with certain tools: You play for the love of the game, nothing else, and you have to respect that always. Your shirt may change, but your responsibilities to those you represent—team, country, race—don't.

At times I have wondered if being from a small Caribbean country worked against me professionally. Sometimes I was certain that it did. There were times when I wondered if going to university robbed me of the valuable early lessons of being a professional footballer. It's at those times that the friendship and experiences of Lincoln "Tiger" Phillips allowed me a better view of what lay ahead, and what had come before. Now I find myself wondering if the game has been better to me than I could ever be to it.

Despite what may seem like higher rewards and hurdles in today's world in general, I truly believe it was immeasurably harder for people like us, from small countries still under-appreciated by the wider world, to make an impact in huge, diverse, and complex countries such as the United States. It was harder still to have that impact resound and uplift an entire race, while making history along the way. And harder yet to have those records stripped from your very grasp, which means starting again from scratch and rebuilding everything, better than it was before. Such is the story of Lincoln and the Howard University Bisons of 1971 and 1974.

I'm not sure where Lincoln holds his accomplishments as Howard University's coach; the pages that follow will reveal that to us, I'm sure. But no one will ever question how high he raised the bar during those years. It was raised even higher by his accomplishments "between the sticks" for country, and for club—in a league that attracted the greatest talents the world had ever seen.

I have been fortunate in who I've had around me my entire life. My father, George, an accomplished athlete and scholar in his own right, continues to be the greatest influence on every aspect of my life, and also my greatest motivation. The stories of his feats are for another day.

As I look for some kind of measure to validate my own life's work I cannot help but find comparison with Lincoln's. Our paths were similar. Though it feels I've heard all about him for as long as I can remember, I only got to know him, the man, more recently. And in getting to know him I have grown more comfortable with not trying to clear the bar he has set, but merely to touch it at full stretch.

Shaka Hislop,
Trinidad and Tobago goalkeeper at World Cup 2006; English First Division and Premier League keeper, 1995-2006

Prologue

As surely as a booted ball returns to earth, the axe was going to fall. I'd coached this African-American university's soccer team to two national championships, winning 116 games against a handful of losses, but without a doubt I'd soon be out of work.

You want to know how I felt? Like the first-rate coach of a first-class team that played a second-class sport. I didn't say soccer was second-class; America did. And so did the man who mattered—Howard University's athletic director Leo Miles. Miles was a former American football player (the kind of football where large men don helmets and tackle head-first), and my success meant nothing to him. My suggestion that the Howard University Bisons men's soccer team be treated the same as the footballers was met with derision.

What did I want? Better soccer boots, a couple paid scouts, an ambulance at home games. I wanted the campus bulletin board to display the soccer team's schedule.

I would air my grievances publicly at the annual athletic banquet—in front of Miles and the Howard University athletic department that had failed to dignify my pleas with a response.

I, Lincoln Abraham Phillips, coach of the proud black Howard University student athletes who had twice proven themselves the best in the country, even with the deck stacked very much against them in 1970s USA. I, Tiger, the leaping, flying Maple goalkeeper who rose to grab shots that most custodians could only punch. I of Queen's Royal College, a prestigious school where a boy of my colour and empty pockets once had no place.

I of the dusty barrack-yard and the hard pavements of St James, Trinidad that wearied under ever-pattering feet as I ran down footballs (is so we does call them in the West Indies) and ran up to bowl at a wicket marked on the side of an outhouse. I of the Trinidad and

Tobago national team that felled the mighty Argentines on the way to bronze at the 1967 Pan Am Games. I of the fledgling professional soccer leagues of the previously soccer-less United States.

I would have my say. Consequences be damned.

1—FLOUR BAG KEEPER

St James, Trinidad, West Indies
1951

Heroes? I had one: His name was Hugh Sealy. Friend, the man could fly! It didn't matter that he kept goal for our rivals, the dreaded Maple. From the very first time I saw the Black Panther dressed in all-black, wearing, oddly enough, a pair of knee-pads, and springing all over to keep our marauding Malvern out of his net, I was hooked. To a nine-year-old sports fanatic going to the Queen's Park Savannah with his big brother to watch fiercely contested First Division football matches for the first time, Sealy was sublime.

And he could flip. The man had springs for Achilles tendons, and he used them to entertain. See the Panther in his box—the slightest crouch and up he goes, heels-over-head and head-over-heels. Back to earth he comes. Upright! Spectators shout. My eyes open wide.

Want to *be* like Panther? Come on! I *was* the Panther. Here come the boys through the streets of St James. A blurry orb is lashed from foot to foot. Each boy, no matter how big or small, clumsy or fleet, is transformed. He becomes his hero.

Mammy cleans house for the wealthy Siegert family of the rum-distilling dynasty, and presses sheets for Chinese clients with an iron heated in a coal pot (always careful to dust off the soot so she doesn't mar those gleaming linens). For me, she boils a flour bag until the writing dissolves. She stitches that bag into a pair of shorts. Along with a long-sleeved white shirt, the flour bag shorts are dunked in darkest dye. Dressed in black socks, black shorts, black shirt, with a pair of socks pulled over my hands as gloves (also black, of course) I prance around at the Woodbrook Youth Centre. Who am I but the Panther?

Until it starts to rain. The puddle beneath me blackens, and my shorts are nothing but a flour bag once again.

No aspirations, man. I was too young for that. Dreams of playing for the national team? Of winning a medal at the Pan Am Games? Of going to the United States to play professional soccer? What you talking 'bout? I just wanted to play, and be the Black Panther.

Our yard at 29 Bengal Street, St James is large. There is plenty room to run and play. Near the entrance from the road is a house, divided into four apartments. Grandpa Dada lives in one, not far from his donkeys, which are penned in the back corner near to my brother's pigeon coop. We have plenty fruit trees—guava, mango, all kinda thing. Obliquely opposite the four apartments is a little shack. That's where I live, with my brother, two sisters and mother.

The house is made of wood. With my face pressed to the gaps between floorboards, I can see packed earth and little clumps of weed. When it rains, the water trickles through the patchwork of galvanize and plexi-glass that we generously call a roof, which means it's time to shift your bed to escape the drip. Never mind the snakes and centipedes that wriggle around overhead; they aren't concerned with you.

In this house, our bellies are full. Mammy is a resourceful woman. Her father, Grandpa Dada, had a deal with a bakery. Mr. Dumbé allowed Dada to cart away baskets of stale bread to feed his donkeys and hogs. With a little water, and heat from our backyard oven, that bread got as soft as freshly baked buns. The pigs don't have a chance. Of course, there's too much for us, so we're off to share with the neighbours.

A yard is a boy's first world. From it, every venture is launched. Ours is the community centre for neighbourhood kids. I can hear Mr. Pinheiro's radio, the only one on the compound. Its tinny Rediffusion[1] broadcast is the soundscape for our cricket games. Big sister Alicia takes two steps and bowls. I swing the bat—too big for my little body. The sound of bat on oil pan wicket is PAM! I tell you; I know it well. "Haha! He out heself!" Have mercy on little Lincoln. Gi' him a next

---

[1]   The only radio frequency in the country at the time, Rediffusion Trinidad re-broadcast BBC programming, supplemented by local news bulletins, live talent and interviews.

chance. PUM! That is the sound of ball on oil pan wicket. The sound that follows is me crying, and everyone else stifling laughter.

If only I could be like Wilbert. My brother was fast and strong. Four years older than me, he was always up to something. If he wasn't tending to his racing pigeons or building cages for his songbirds, he kept a sharp eye out for opportunity. Down the road he comes one day, looking as tall as a moko jumbie to me.[2] Behind him trails a rope. At the end is a large goat. The beast was roaming the streets. It looked lost and ownerless, so naturally Wilbert decided he better bring it home for safekeeping. The poor ruminant belonged to a man who lived a few houses away.

And if Dada slipped, Wilbert made him smell hell. Like the time the old man brought home a huge bunch of bananas from my uncle's farm and hung it to ripen in the untenanted apartment next to his. The bunch was six feet tall at least, and too much temptation for Wilbert and me to avoid. When Dada noticed that it was missing hands, he took out the hammer and nails. BAM! BAM! BAM! He boarded up the door. But Dada, you forget about the window?

Here comes Cokey-o-ko, as the scout ladder was known. Wilbert laces his fingers behind his back so I can step into the rung, stand on his shoulder and slide through the apartment window. Inside, I cut off two hands of bananas and retreat. This goes on for days. Now comes Dada to claim his fruit. I am up in the guava tree, watching him pry off the nails. What he sees inside is the skeleton of a bunch, a six-foot-long stem with no fruit on it. The bellow hits me like a thunderclap: "WHERE MY . . . !" Dada tumbles into the yard with fire rippling from his ears, and I dart off to warn Wilbert that the old man is on the hunt, intent on warming his backside. For a week during daylight hours, Wilbert cannot be found.

I spent my fair share of time with Dada, a tall, good-looking Barbadian who lived by himself but never lacked a woman's touch. We'd leave St James on his donkey cart and clop along towards the capital, Port-of-Spain, where we made the rounds of Chinese restaurants, collecting leftovers and vegetable trimmings to feed the hogs. The donkey knows the way home—left on Park Street, right on Colville, past Astor Cinema, left on Roberts, right on Damien, left on

---

[2]   A stilt-walking Carnival character.

the Western Main Road, back to Bengal Street—so it isn't a problem if Dada drinks too much and falls asleep.

For years it confused me to watch Dada carefully weigh the pork he was selling, wrap it in paper, and then flick on a few extra pieces. It was some time before Wilbert revealed that Dada only did this for his "friends"—an array of not-so-lonely women.

My father liked women, too. It was not uncommon at the time for men in our neighbourhood to have multiple families. My father did, and so he was divided. There was Mom in St James with her four children, Mrs. Howard in Woodbrook with two, and Ms. Luanne, known to us as Tant Lu, who had one boy. I saw my father on Tuesdays and Sunday mornings when he made the rounds to visit his families. He worked for the Port-of-Spain City Council and was a regular at the Green Coconut Tree and Brooklyn bars. If ever I needed him, I walked to his watering holes and looked for his bike outside. After I'd achieved some fame in local football circles, he often drank for free.

Dad was a handy sort of fellow, and creative in his own way. The public statues around Port-of-Spain were a standard copper-green until he got the job to paint them. On some of those jobs, he took me along to hand him his brushes and paints. He transformed Lord Harris, a 19th century governor of Trinidad, by painting him in colours that corresponded more closely to real life. Christopher Columbus got similar treatment. The jobs were good for me: I got to be near him and my pockets jangled with change.

He was a small, musical man who liked to "pull bass" at Carnival time, trotting around town, drinking grog and making music with his good partner Lumpy. He made his big, four-string bass guitars himself; a new one each year. The man was clever. It seemed to me that he could build anything. The only thing he never messed with was electricity.

I liked my Carnival too. The boys contort with laughter when I show up on roller skates to play a sailor mas with Del Vikings, our St James Carnival band. They knew I could skate, but no one else in costume was rolling on eight wheels. Outside of Carnival, our little skating gang terrorized St James. Speed! Our locomotive devices were cobbled together from disparate makes of skates. A boy might combine a Phillips frame with Winchester wheels; it mattered not the hybrid, once it rolled. And every afternoon it was off to the gas station to root through the trash cans for oil. Freshly oiled and powered by legs that never tired, it was time to race.

Carnival always found us competing for ol' mas[3] prize money at the Chinese and Portuguese associations. My best caricature was of a famous West Indies fast bowler with a notoriously long run-up. Wearing a short dress and cricket boots, I let some air out of a basketball and tucked it up inside the dress over my belly. With my hard, knobby knees and slightly bowed legs adding to the get-up, the crowd at the judging venue went wild when I turned around, revealing the sign on my back: "Wes Hall about to deliver."[4]

Since Dad didn't live with us, Mammy was responsible for daily discipline. She had her hands full with Wilbert and me, even when we meant well. We'd been admiring our neighbour's garden, full of gerberas of different hues when we decided Mammy needed a flowerbed too. We dug up a nice big bed in the yard, adding manure from Dada's donkeys into the mix. Glistening with water, it looked as if a tropical profusion would spontaneously burst forth. The obvious answer to the question of where the plants should come from was Mr. Clifford. Over the fence we crept and uprooted his gerberas. We woke early next day hoping to see Mammy smile. The gerberas were happy enough, their petals bobbing in the sunshine. Blood filled Mammy's eyes. Wilbert suffered an immediate case of the "hammer hammers." As he retreated from our mother's glare, all that fell from his slack jaw was "hammer, hammer . . ." I claimed total ignorance as she ordered that the plants be returned before she returned from work.

As we waited for nightfall to reverse Operation Gerbera, the plaintive voice of Clifford's maid wafted into our yard. "Mr. Clifford, like somebody steal the plants?" On seeing her empty flowerbed next day, our mother called us to her. "I understand what you were trying to do," she said as she hugged us both, "but that is stealing. If you want something, you ask." Meanwhile, the neighbour's maid was calling for her boss: "Mr. Clifford, the plants come back!"

---

3   A tradition of satirizing topical issues and personalities while dressed in home-made costumes.

4   A bowler's ball is also known as a "delivery."

My mother was very much a West Indian woman. She believed that sparing the rod meant spoiling the child. Supergoodman, a thick leather belt, hung menacingly from a nail over Wilbert's cot. The hiss of his name was all that was required to invoke mass hysteria. One day, after Wilbert had suffered a particularly good cutass,[5] we decided action was called for. Mammy left for work. We doused Supergoodman in kerosene, flicked a match on him, and dumped his charred remains in the outdoor latrine. It wasn't long before his services were required, but Mammy's scrabbling fingers met only bare nail. Out of sight, we snickered. Supergoodman's reign of terror had ended.

I was coming along physically by now. Although I was nowhere near the 6'1" 170-pound frame that gave me the stature to be a professional goalkeeper, I was no longer the smallest, least coordinated, budding sportsman in St James. But I still hadn't settled on my sport. I'd try anything.

The illustrious Mannie Dookie, the first athlete to represent Trinidad at an international sports meet, running the three—and six-mile events barefoot on a cinder track that cut his 19-year-old feet to shreds at the British Empire Games of 1934, lived on Kandahar Street, not far from us. I went to his home and gawked at the distance-running trophies lining his walls and filled my belly with his wife's cooking. Mannie urged all the neighbourhood prospects to meet him at King George V Park where the Dookie School trained. It was there that he forced me into an early retirement from competitive distance-running.

"Give her a ten-yard headstart," instructs Mannie, urging a girl named Babby to inch forward. "Ready, set, go!" Too soon, I am coming around the final bend where Mannie orders me to close the gap. The afterburners ignite. My back arches. "Close the gap!" insists the coach. Arms flail as effort translates to ugliness, and I cross the finish line in a shower of derision exactly ten yards adrift. I consider myself retired even before the picong[6] begins. "Boy, he thought Babby was kneeling down. All he could see was the sole of she foot!"

I was getting to know my half-brothers through sports as well. Winston and Euan, Dad's sons with Mrs. Howard, both played cricket. They were younger than me by several years and once I started

---

[5]   Spanking.

[6]   Heckling.

batting they could seldom get me out. Soon enough, however, I found that I couldn't get *them* out. It turned out that they'd been training with a club in Cocorite.

There was only so much my mother could do with reheated bread and flour bags. She eventually made the financial decision to send Alicia, her eldest, to live with an uncle in Maraval. Wilbert went to the farm in Diego Martin with Uncle Sonny, where Dada's hogs were kept. I stayed at home in St James with my mother and little sister Marilyn, the family spoil chile.[7]

By now, I was a sportsman. When I visited Wilbert at the farm, darkness found me outside the house, the ball bouncing off my foot as I kept it aloft. BUP BUP BUP BUMP. Start over. BUP BUP BUP BUP BUP BUP . . . When Wilbert can be found, I make him shoot the ball at me from a few yards away. He kicks when my back is turned. It soon becomes a game. In the murky light, I spin and catch the ball. "You's a bat!" says Wilbert. "Only bat could see in the dark!"

The farm proved good for conditioning, too. While living there I met track athlete Edwin Roberts. On mornings before school, we ran several miles to Carenage where we often took a dip in the grey Gulf of Paria before running home. Edwin was fast enough that he could easily have left me, but he never did. By 1964, when I was starting in net for the national football team, on the cusp of the country's first-ever World Cup qualifying match, Edwin had proven that those morning runs and countless laps of the sand track at the Queen's Park Savannah had done him well. He won two bronze—in the 200 metre and 4X400 m relay—at the Summer Olympics in Japan.

I was no slouch at any sport I put my mind to. After the Harlem Globetrotters came to town to show off their skills, I got a basketball. It was my companion, like Tom Hanks's volleyball Wilson in *Cast Away*. We slept together, and I spent all my time spinning that ball on my fingers and imitating the Globetrotters' impossibly agile clowning. Dad's son with Aunt Lu, Georgie, was on a basketball team, and he showed me how to keep my elbow pointed straight at the basket when I shot. Before that, it had pretty much been 'heave-ho and hope it go.' I improved so much under Georgie's tutelage and with regular playing time in a budding league that I was destined for the national team.

---

[7]   Coddled child.

My days of kites, marbles, and roller skating in Carnival costume were drawing to a close. And my first big football match was already behind me. That was the day I saved for my primary school, St Crispin's, looking as sharp as The Panther until the rain came down and washed the illusion away.

2—The bench of the Bays

Queen's Park Savannah, Trinidad 1962

No time for recriminations: Here comes "Buggy" Haynes, steaming down the wing like a man who has just disturbed a jep[8] nest and has no intention of being stung. With all my Regiment defenders soundly beaten, I have to deal with this torment alone. Off the line I come to narrow the angle. As the Malvern forward lights his cannon, blasting the ball far-post to my right, I am leaning left. Somehow (don't ask how; I still don't know) I reversed my momentum and got enough hand on the shot to push it wide. A good thing too, since we were 1-0 up with only ten minutes left in the match. A place in the FA final was at stake.

With Malvern throwing caution to the wind, my defence did its best to keep the marauders in check. The fans in the packed Queen's Park Oval were losing their minds, screaming support and shouting curses in equal measure. Over the din, I shouted instructions at my defenders. I really didn't want to deal with Buggy one-on-one again. When the next shot came, however, it wasn't him. It was Franklyn Olliviere who had hammered the ball up toward the 'V', where the crossbar meets the upright. This wasn't one to punch or push. Hit with authority, from far enough out that I saw it coming, I leapt, upwards and sideways, grabbed the sizzling sphere and drew it to my chest, like a man embracing his lover. I returned to earth knowing—if that one didn't beat me, nothing passing here to-day! Olliviere later told me it was the best piece of goalkeeping he'd ever seen.

---

[8]   Hornet.

My team, Regiment, held on to win that match 1-0. And we won the FA final that followed. But the moment that changed the course of my life came not long after those two saves against Buggy and Olliviere. Someone told me that sportscaster Raffi Knowles, who had done the live radio commentary, had sent a message: A scout for an American pro-soccer team wanted to meet me at the Hilton Hotel.

On Raffi's advice, scout Derek Tomkinson had gone to the Oval to see me play. He was very impressed with my second-half saves and wanted to sign me to the Baltimore Bays for the 1968 season. The Bays played in the fledgling North American Soccer League. Left to me, a man named *Lincoln Abraham*, I'd have jumped on the plane to the United States immediately.

My mother admired the Americans; perhaps because she was a hard worker herself. Breaking her back as a domestic servant in the homes of the wealthy and washing sheets at home after hours, she saw the bareback Yankee soldiers sweating it out in the tropical heat and she thought to herself: Them fellas good. We were a British colony, you see, and the Brits had granted their American allies enough land in Trinidad's northwest peninsula to build a large military base to protect the Allies' interest during World War II.

The Caribbean was a theatre of war, with German U-boats patrolling the murky depths, and T&T had oil reserves that needed close watch. Caribbean military bases were also stopping the Germans from moving into the Gulf of Mexico where the Americans were producing the fuel that powered the war machine. In the course of protecting T&T's precious fuel, the Americans developed our infrastructure. Very much in the public view, the soldiers worked on our roads and highways. When I was born, on July 4, 1941, the day of America's independence—Mom had decided I would carry the name of the U.S. president who had freed the slaves. Not Abraham Lincoln, but Lincoln Abraham.

With a name like that, what could I tell Derek Tomkinson? That I didn't want to play professional football, or 'soccer' as the Yankees called it, in the good old U.S. of A? That I wanted to serve out the sixth and final year of my Regiment contract and keep my sergeant's stripes? As long as Tomkinson could guarantee that the Baltimore Bays would pay for my continued education, Lincoln Abraham was heading north. The scout assured that he could arrange it. My wife Linda would have to agree, but I shook Tomkinson's hand, already relatively certain that I'd go. I signed a one-year contract for US $7,000, which sounded like a lot of money until I arrived in the States.

Jamaica was the first stop. Tomkinson was living on the island and the Bays trained there in the pre-season. Having played in leagues where I knew most of the players personally, these first training sessions were a shock. I didn't know a single player. These white boys were big and strong, with calves as thick as the trunks of young flamboyants. When I shook hands with the starting goalie, mine was swallowed up. It took a pair of Jamaicans, twins Art and Asher Welch, to relieve my anxiety. "Dem is saps," said one of the two. "I go salad dem," crowed the other. Imagine my relief when I saw the fearsome physical specimens having the ball repeatedly passed through their legs (a footballer's ultimate humiliation) by the Jamaican twins who had promised 'salad' for lunch. On the long training runs, my new friends encouraged me, and I often finished in the top three; right behind the twins.

My first few weeks in Baltimore, I lived rent-free with Art and Asher at the Wakefield Apartments, a housing complex for professional athletes including the American football players of the Baltimore Colts, the basketballers of the Baltimore Bullets, and the baseball players of the Orioles. But who told me to offer to put gas in the brothers' old American banger? The car guzzled it, belched, and demanded more.

When we could get a scratchy connection, Linda and I spoke by phone. But the calls often dropped mid-sentence leaving me even more frustrated and homesick than I already was. I missed her, and my little boys.

At the Bays, starting goalkeeper Terry Adlington, the man with the giant hands, was traded to Dallas before the 1968 season began. Hope flickered that I would start. It was extinguished when coach Gordon Jago, former manager of English club Queen's Park Rangers, announced that the Bays had signed Spanish goalkeeper Carmelo Cedrún. Carmelo had played two matches for Spain at the World Cup in Chile six years earlier and had fourteen years' professional experience with Spanish professional club Athletic Bilbao. I had played for amateur first division teams and my country (a speck on your world map) at the Pan Am Games. He was going to start; I would warm the bench. The only question was for how long.

I sat on that bench for twenty-six matches. Twenty-six matches of pure agony. Two thousand three hundred and forty minutes of celebrating every goal we scored and hanging my head for every one scored against us. (Although I couldn't help feeling tiny bursts of pleasure whenever Carmelo let in a soft one.) He was 38, and past his prime. I was 27, fit, and as agile as I'd ever be. At training, with a small crowd watching, I gave them the Tiger Show—springing to grab or punch even when a leap wasn't needed. I think it intimidated Carmelo. He knew that behind-the-scenes, players were lobbying for me to save.

At a Meet the Bays banquet, Coach Jago introduced me as one of the only players who hadn't played. With microphone in hand, I warned him politely: "If you make the mistake and put me in net, I'm not coming out."

By the time Jago put me in, we had a losing record and no chance of making the playoffs. Professional soccer was clinging to life in the United States and Jago knew the Bays would probably be disbanded. He later said that he wanted to give me a chance to be picked up somewhere else. With six games left in the season, I got a start, eager to make an impression on anyone who saw me.

My first professional game, on August 11, 1968 against the Kansas City Spurs, started dreadfully. Inside the first few minutes, Kansas City striker Eric Barber lobbed one towards goal. What possessed me to try to push the ball over the bar, I'll never know. All I managed was to palm it weakly into the net. With the laughter of the Kansas City home fans ringing in my ears, I hoped for an earthquake to open a crack large enough to swallow me whole. It was only the calm words of skipper Dennis Viollet, a survivor of the 1958 plane crash that killed eight of his Manchester United teammates that got me through the half. I surrendered one more that game, and we lost 2-1.

Yet the Baltimore press was kind. (Maybe because I'd cultivated quite a few sports reporters who knew little to nothing about the "foreign" game. I always took the time to explain the game's intricacies—not with any payback in mind, but because I hoped the sport would grow with exposure.) The headline on the match report read: "K.C. TOPS BAYS, BUT PHILLIPS LOOKS GREAT

IN DEBUT." The reporter wrote that I had stopped "a point-blank four-yarder," and just got a hand to "a 25-yarder that whacked off the crossbar."

It was not until my third match that I tasted my first professional win, over the Boston Beacons in front of 2,393 at Baltimore Memorial Stadium. My friends in the media said I'd had a "remarkably stunning day":

"Early in the second period, the rangy Trinidad native came out fast to deflect a point-blank shot by Yilma Ketema. Later, he dove to his right to save a hard, whistling shot from 15 yards out by Rijzenburg. Less than a minute later, he sprinted from the net to smother an attempt by Erik Dyreborg."

It had taken long enough to get a breakthrough, and already my abbreviated six-game season was halfway through. But Linda had joined me from Trinidad, which meant, among other things, that I ate better. She also brought our sons Sheldon and Sean up with her. Money, however, was still as tight as tight could be. In Trinidad we'd say "I broken to tief,"[9] but I hadn't stolen anything since Wilbert and I had helped ourselves to Mr. Clifford's gerberas. Part-time work refereeing youth matches at $10 a pop kept my head above water; school kept me motivated.

I was not leaving the United States without a qualification in Physical Education. I'd already been sent on a physical training course in England, courtesy the T&T Regiment, and now I was enrolled at the "illustrious" Catonsville Community College of Baltimore. I was older, and of darker complexion, than the average Catonsville student, and I sat around for almost a semester hearing the occasional reference to "dem niggers" as well as disparaging remarks about the Civil Rights movement.

These were fraught times. Months after I arrived, Martin Luther King had been assassinated and Baltimore had gone up in flames as African-Americans vented their grief and anger on the city. I'd been at the cinema with the Jamaican twins when the movie was interrupted by a breaking news flash that King had been shot. We walked out

---

[9]   I'm so broke, I could steal.

of the theatre to see smoke rising in the distance. The burning and looting had begun.

My Catonsville classmates were usually conscious of my presence, pausing to exempt me whenever they made a racist reference. "Not you, Lincoln. You're different." When I couldn't take it anymore, I stood up and lectured them, saying there were good black people and bad ones, just as there were good and bad whites. I urged them to consider which type of whites they were. Every man went silent. I won't say that race talk never arose after that, but I certainly didn't hear as much of it.

The Bays barely survived to play in the 1969 season in a shrunken North American Soccer League, but I was no longer part of the team. But all that sitting on the bench next to coach Jago had paid off. He so respected my tactical insight that he recommended me as player-coach to the manager of the Washington Darts, a semi-professional team playing in the American Soccer League, which, unfortunately, was also struggling.

Football, basketball, baseball—that's been the sporting hierarchy in the U.S. since way back when. Soccer is in a relatively good position today with a professional league that attracts aging superstars and promising young players who sometimes break through to the more lucrative European leagues, but in the 60s, the sport was just carving out a niche. The fan and player bases were found mostly in the immigrant communities. Since the sport was being played on the fringes, the money was small. To coach *and* play for the Darts, I made $3,000 for the season. Linda yelled her lungs out in the stands. A win earned me a precious $200 bonus.

Among six Trinidadians to join me at the Darts were Gerry Brown and solid defender Victor Gamaldo. Victor and I had played football in Trinidad from school days to the national team, and became fast friends (or conspirators in courting) when he came to make a move behind Linda's younger sister—the woman he eventually married. I had learnt his name during a match for the Port of Spain Football League B team. I was 17, playing out of net, and enjoyed brilliant direct-to-foot service (which allowed me to bag about four) from a smaller teammate. That was Victor. He was only 14-years-old.

In the absence of female care in the United States, Victor once burnt off his eyebrows with a clumsy attempt at lighting our gas stove.

On the field, however, he was smooth, and we communicated well without having to say much. He remains as close as family today.

Meanwhile, I was still in school at Catonsville. Some of the words in my Anatomy classes were so long my eyelids drooped before I could even finish saying them, but I was bumbling through; at least until the Trinidad and Tobago Football Federation (T&TFF) called for Victor, Gerry Brown and me to come home to play for the national team. Foolishly, I dropped out of school and packed my bags before the federation decided that we were asking for too much money and told us not to come. (They claimed that I had asked for $2,500, when the truth was that all I requested was $250 to pay my rent in the U.S. while I was gone.) By the time the federation's invitation was rescinded, it was too late to start classes.

I was well on the road to becoming a tramp athlete—the type of professional sportsman who lives from meal to meal until he leaps to grab a ball and comes down awkwardly, injuring his knee and jeopardizing his livelihood. My referee's license was earning me some money, but I couldn't see myself making a career of it. By now, I knew I was destined to coach. The minimum professional qualification, apart from the coaching certificates I'd go on to earn, was a degree in Physical Education.

Bowie State University, a black college in Maryland just east of Washington DC, took me in as a Phys Ed student. Not only did they accept my credits, they also gave me a job coaching the soccer team. And what a dreadful bunch of misfits they were. Chick, our big fat goalkeeper, fell to earth in slow motion several hours after the ball had passed him and nestled quietly in the back of the net. In a match against University of Maryland, Baltimore County (UMBC) where we were slaughtered 13-0, I heard a female spectator exclaim: "Oh Gawd, that guy is horrrrrrible." She was looking directly at Chick. The humiliation was compounded when the UMBC coach walked over and lectured my players. Don't get discouraged, he urged. The man had no idea how much danger he was in. I sat on my hands, swallowing hard. I, Abraham Lincoln Phillips, didn't have the first clue how I was going to make a silk purse out of this rather tatty sow's ear, but I did know that there had to be better athletes at Bowie.

My first stop was the basketball team, where I found a competitive fellow by the name of Hamilton Holder. With a little coaching, he ended up at centre-back. Scrounging diligently, I found a couple Africans, an Armenian who nobody liked, and a tall, white drug addict. I put him in goal to replace Chick. BAM! We won a game. For the return match against UMBC, the team was psyched up, and we blanked them 1-0. As we walked off the field, one of my players called over to the UMBC bench: "Coach, thanks for the tip. We trained real hard." When the athletic director heard that we'd won, he instructed me to take the gang for a meal. "No hamburgers, Coach. Steak."

Class was another challenge. I'm what you'd call a kinesthetic learner, meaning that I pick things up when I can perform some kind of physical activity to illustrate the lesson. I've never been much good at listening to lectures. Outside of class, I got some help from a former teacher from Trinidad. Kelvin Joseph somehow translated Anatomy and Physiology into stories that stuck. To grasp basic anatomy, I found a fourth-grade book with a colourful illustration of blood flowing through the body. I was starting to understand that people have different learning styles. Some prefer listening; others need to see or touch. For a coach, it translates simply: Players learn in different ways.

At home, we'd taken the difficult decision to send our two boys to Trinidad to live with Linda's parents. We knew it would only last until we got on firmer financial footing, but it took a toll on Linda. Her stomach hurt something terrible and doctors couldn't diagnose the problem. I, however, knew exactly what it was: While I had been studying, coaching the Darts, and refereeing matches, she had far too much time to think about her sons.

Victor, Gerry and I were in the U.S. on work visas (H-1) that allowed us to play soccer, and we'd initiated the process of applying for permanent residency. Whenever we looked for extra work, we were violating the terms of our visas and taking a huge risk. But there was no getting around it; we really needed the money, especially if we wanted to go back to Trinidad for Christmas. In Baltimore, we worked shifts at Olde's Envelope Factory where we stacked envelopes in boxes and assembled cartons. The plant managers thought so much of us that they offered to move us up to operating a guillotine-type device that came down with a KANG!, severing a two-foot-high stack of paper. I still needed my hands for my day job, so I politely declined the promotion.

My other job in Baltimore was at the bleach and dye factory. Mine was the monotonous task of directing the cloth on its way to being dyed. It seemed to flow forever, like water over a fall, and I soon fell asleep. When the falls gurgled and sputtered, I woke to see the cloth bunching up on the rack. Leaping for the control panel, I tripped on some wires, adding to the racket. The manager stormed in, pushed me aside and shut down the show. Surveying the mangled cloth and the dye-covered floor, he muttered words that scorched my eardrums. "#%$&! #%$&! #%$&! I've never seen anything like this before."

After lunch, he handed me a scrubbing brush, a pair of tall rubber boots and a bucket of liquid soap for a job he claimed I "couldn't mess up." I was dispatched to a grime-caked trough. It was twenty feet long and ten feet deep at least. Standing over that foul chasm, I started to cry. Look at you, Lincoln Phillips: You left your good army job to come to America *for this*! Look what you come to.

3—ME, AT QRC

Queen's Park Savannah, Trinidad 1958

The man had a good eye for talent. You could often find him meandering across the patchy grass of the Queen's Park Savannah—a small "Chinee" man wheeling his bicycle. His little wooden bench is perched atop the seat. Meet Pa Aleong, *pro bono* trainer of promising footballers and cricketers.

Pa's sons went to St Mary's College, an all-boys high school, so much of his attention was devoted to the boys in the baby blue school shirts. I wore the dark blue shirt of Queen's Royal College (QRC); really, he had no business coaching me. Yet he did.

While goalkeeping for QRC one day, I went to fetch a ball that had been booted past the goal. Pa, who was sitting in the stands, leaned over and commented: "Lincoln, you dropping balls on your left side." Before sunrise the next day, I was hustling through St James on my way to an appointment at King George V Park. No rocket science in the remedy for left-side laxity; just Pa, standing in the park, knocking balls to my left, again and again and again.

Pa Aleong had never kept goal in his life, but he understood balance and movement. His sons were skilful players, and I was lucky to be picked for Pa's informal coaching academy. I believe it was because I showed promise and took his advice without question. But not all his counsel was accepted. Walking past President's House one day, Pa trundled over to a group of boys harassing a ball and offered some pearls of wisdom. As a barrage of invective rained down on his head, he turned tail and scampered to safety.

Me—I devoured every ounce of advice Pa doled out. There was no specialized goalkeeping coaching in Trinidad in those days, so I foraged for tips in every nook and cranny. At the T&T Football Association headquarters on Abercromby Street, I stood beneath the "Know the Game" charts from England, studying the pictures on the correct way to dive, punch, and kick.

Even when I moved up to First Division football in my late teens, Pa still found time for me. If I was having a problem with balls flighted in from the wings, that was what we focused on. There was no deviating from his schedule. After I'd graduated from secondary school, he once set a training session that clashed with the Intercol[10] final. Pa's two charges that day, both playing for Maple football club at the time, were graduates of the bitter college rivals who were playing each other. Sedley Joseph badly wanted to see St Mary's stomp all over QRC; I wanted to see QRC hammer the smug "Saints" into the Savannah pitch. Pa had other ideas. From a small grove of palms in the middle of the Savannah, we could hear the cheers and groans of the crowd as Pa drilled us; neither of us knowing which school held the advantage.

Who can say why the pursuit of a ball fascinated me so? I can only surmise that there is pleasure in the movement of the body and joy in competition. They say that scientists have identified a rush of pleasing hormones that bathes the brain when the heart beats faster and blood rushes through the human body. Beyond this, who doesn't enjoy doing something that they're good at? I was good at football and I played a lot of it.

My first foray outside of school football came with a First Division amateur club. Providence had lost their keeper and the team was trying out a couple new prospects. I was 16-years-old. On my first tryout, I didn't get many shots and Providence selected a guy named Potter as their custodian. Me, I got picked as a striker, and Dad coughed up the ten cent club membership fee. Potter quickly proved his lack of talent, so the Providence captain approached me in the Savannah the day before a big match. "Ay, glad to see you," he said. "You playing Sunday." I did not own a pair of soccer shoes.

As I ran out in front of the fans on Sunday in borrowed cleats a half-size too small, I thought I might defecate. Thank God for

---

[10] Inter-college—the high school championship match.

Arthur Belgrave, a strapping central defender. "Son, anything in the air is mine," commanded Arthur B. "You stay home." The first ball that came across the goal, I understood why. As everyone jumped in unison, his waist drew level with their heads. And he headed the ball as if he had kicked it. "Arthur B!" he shouted, and I knew he had it under control. (This was back in the day, before goalkeepers were protected from over-aggressive tackling by changes in the rules. Running into the keeper was fair play. I eventually learnt to protect myself from flying forwards by sticking out my bottom or tucking my knees when I jumped. Take that bottom and them knees!)

The match began in a blur, with a ball ricocheting off the post and into my arms. Another came off the crossbar. Somewhere in between, I saved a couple good ones. At the final whistle, we were up 1-0.

"You did good," said Eddie Farrell, one of the guys from the block in my community. "But you must always know where you are." Farrell, aloof and well-respected in the neighbourhood, had noticed that I needed help with positioning. "Measure the mid-point of the goal," he said. "Take six paces out, and put a mark." He promised that from his magic spot, I could close a shooter's angle by drifting to either side.

After that, I always found a scrap of paper or cigarette box to mark my X. I was the first goalkeeper in the country to do it, and Farrell was the man who showed me how. It worked well until Paragon's coach figured me out and had his forwards kick my mark away as soon as they entered the box. Damn, it messed me up; at least until I realized that digging a hole with my heel also did the job.

My Old Man was friendly with Clarence Burke, which meant I didn't pay school fees at Burke's College, a private school that neither of my parents could otherwise afford. When the very proper Mr. Burke, a polished man who used merciless Standard English and called his students "little asses" for foolish behaviour, abruptly closed the school, I found myself looking for somewhere to complete my high school education. I had just turned 16.

Fatima College had recently opened, so I tried there first. No luck. Onto St Mary's College, who were often secondary school football champions. The school, run by Catholic priests, also enjoyed a reputation for producing scholarship-winning students. I really didn't have the academic lustre to attend, but my mother was encouraging.

"Anywhere you want to go," she urged, "you could go." With this in mind, and the confidence I'd gained from starting in net for Providence, I approached the college principal and told him I'd like to play for the senior side. "We have a very good team," Father Valdez informed me icily. "Anybody would like to play for us."

I headed for Queen's Royal College to try again. Still rattling around my cranium was a disparaging remark made by the mother of a friend from Burke's: "QRC! You can't get into QRC!" My mother, however, had told me simply: "You go. Talk to them."

QRC's main building is an imposing, maroon-coloured structure that looks out onto the Savannah where I played many of my games. Not quite as snooty as St Mary's, the school boasted a long list of distinguished alumni: our island's first prime minister Dr. Eric Williams, Nobel literature laureate V.S. Naipaul, and intellectual giant—author, philosopher and political thinker—CLR James. They played some decent football, and my friends from St Crispin's Primary School in St James, Tony Campbell and the roving bunch of never-sit-still sportsmen, also went there. There, at least, I had a reference. College sports master Rex Dewhurst, a big white guy who also dressed in white, managed the Port of Spain League's Second Team, which I had played on. Dewhurst also had some QRC students, my teammates from the "soft-shoe" soccer league,[11] whispering in his ears to admit me. He referred me to the principal.

Write me an essay, said Mr. Mitchell, on why you want to attend QRC. I wrote about walking past the college and seeing the students playing football in the field right behind their classrooms. I wrote about yearning to join them. (Burke's didn't have its own grounds, so we had to walk a fair distance to the Savannah to play.) "This is well-written," said Mitchell, surveying my earnest offering. "A lot of passion." He tapped his pencil on the edge of the desk. "A few grammatical errors, but we can fix that." No sooner had he said "You're into QRC" than I was off to find my father, who was paving the road for the City Council. "Oh Gawd," he said, pacing to and fro. "I have to get the money."

Money—it was always short, yet I never wanted for anything. Back came my father with enough for the khaki pants, shirt, and

---

[11]   The soft-shoe league was played in shoes that had rubber pegs. It was the premier league for boys younger than 14. Our team was Starlets.

diagonally-striped two-tone blue tie, which I bought, as everyone else did, at Glendennings uniform store. But a uniform wasn't the only essential. It was cricket season, and the unfortunate consequence of somehow getting bat to a wildly swinging ball during team tryouts was that I made the team. Now I needed cricket whites.[12]

Mr. Bhagan, St James tailor, told me to come to his shop to get measured. Bhagan knew me from playing for Upsetters, a cricket team comprised mostly of East Indians from St James. Free of charge, he presented me with a pair of white drill pants and a pair of flannels. Uncle Sonny, my mother's brother, decided that I should have the $35 shoes instead of the $12 pair, and when I got to the sports store, the owner screwed in extra studs. "You have to play well," he insisted, and each peg he tightened was a prayer for my success. All I needed now was a white flannel shirt, so Mum stripped off her jewelry and told me to pawn it. "Everybody have those shirts," she said. "You have to have one too."

I was no stranger to benevolence. My older sister Alicia had given me my first pair of football shorts. They were hers, and had a zip on the side. When I came home caked in mud, Alicia scrubbed my clothes clean. She also bought me my first pair of football boots. They were Adidas, and getting them was like being given a brand-new car. Between uses, I polished them with Kiwi (rather than the inferior Nugget), and massaged them with Dubbin leather protector. I loosened each peg and applied a tiny drop of oil so the screws wouldn't rust. At night, I woke to look at them, perched on the shelf of our shack.

At the college, for some inscrutable reason, I was placed in Five Science, where I quickly demonstrated my academic mediocrity. As football season came around, I was looking for gaps where I could steal a spot on the senior team. The keeper, McGregor Hinkson, had locked up his job with a rusty old chain, so I told the coach I played central defense, where a spot had opened up.

Let me attempt to convey the hype surrounding college football in those days. Each school called an assembly on big game days to present its team. The players were paraded in the courtyard before hundreds of adrenalin-pumped young men, knowing that the honour

---

[12]   A cricket uniform—traditionally all-white.

of the establishment would soon rest at their feet. Students roared and horns blared.

At QRC in the 1950s, the boy who became the country's foremost designer of Carnival costumes, Peter Minshall, saved up his pocket money to buy blue fabric that he sewed together into a giant school banner. With no small degree of pride, he painted QUEEN'S ROYAL COLLEGE across the flag in yellow and orange Chinese lacquer. The celebration that year was so exuberant that Minshall and his schoolmates were arrested while feteing[13] in the streets.

In 1959, with me playing stopper just in front of goalkeeper Hinkson, we faced our rivals St Mary's in the Intercol final. The match had been advertised on the radio for weeks in advance. "Once a year in October!" went the jingle. "Big fete in Queen's Park Savannah!" The warm-up began in the QRC gymnasium, before the entire team was packed into a few cars and driven the couple miles around the Savannah to the Grand Stand. The crowd was thick, and as we approached, the bugles and drums washed over us. As we clattered out of the dressing room, the swollen crowd bellowed. The iron[14] of the rhythm section clanked away, and the hypnotic chant began: "QRC! We want a goal!"

Knotted up at nil, St Mary's slipped the ball past Hinkson, who was off his line. It dribbled along as quickly as a morrocoy[15] fleeing a torrent of molasses and seemed to settle in the groove of the goal line, rotating with agonizing slowness. My teammate Tony Campbell (a friend from the soft-shoe leagues who was not blessed with blazing speed) graciously escorted it. A decade passed before he managed to clear. In the second half, I went up for a header that I deflected past the upright. I also missed the next attacking header I tried for, but my teammate Billy Samuel was there to nod it in. We went on to win 2-0.

The return to QRC around the Savannah (billed today as the world's largest roundabout) was mas.[16] Over the loudspeaker, in a packed yard, they called the names of every player on the team. Mine, I felt, was announced more loudly than anyone else's.

---

13   Partying; in this case, to the sound of iron percussion instruments.

14   Typically, car wheel hubs and cow bells beaten with iron rods.

15   Tortoise.

16   The noise and energy associated with the festival of Carnival.

But it was on the cricket pitch, dressed in the white uniform provided by an entire community, that I made a lasting impact.

"See Wembley and die." That's what sports fans used to say about England's 90,000-seat stadium. When I walked into the Queen's Park Oval at the age of 18 to play the Intercol cricket final of 1959, I finally understood what they meant about a venue's ability to inspire awe. This was sacred ground, played upon by West Indies cricketers whose boots I would gladly have cared for as lovingly as I did my own.

Anxious and fired up for the match, my very first for QRC, I arrived early. Looking out on the meticulously kept expanse of green, the mountains of the Northern Range rising in the background, I began to sweat, perspiration flowing down my back like the first rainy season shower tumbling down the East Dry River.

All the boys from the area had turned up to see me play. We won the toss and chose to bat. I had been picked as an opening batsman, but captain Henley Wooding must have sensed my anxiety (maybe the rivers of sweat betrayed me) and pushed me down the order. St Mary's soon had us on the back foot—25 runs for 3 wickets, 36 for 4, 50 for 5. Henley kept delaying my entrance, and the anticipation of being sent in was doing nothing to calm my nerves. When the skipper sent me in at #7, I picked up my heavy Frank Worrell bat and descended the hallowed steps with churning stomach. "Who's dat fella?" asked a spectator. "I doh know," came the response. "We go soon find out."

The first ball was on the pads, and I used Old Frank to clobber it through the onside for a boundary. Then I tickled another for three. Anything on the legs was food. Years of cricket in the road—with the wicket chalked up on the side of a latrine, and in-swing created by the treacherous curve of a curbside cutout—had prepared me for onside bowling. Soon, the Saints were forced to spread the field. Ellery Jones, the competent senior bat at the other end of the wicket suggested that we start dropping the ball for quick singles. By the time we retired,[17] we'd put on almost 100.

In the St Mary's innings, I snapped up a few catches at slip. But it was at mid-wicket that I fielded the ball I'll never forget. Running and tumbling, I took what appeared to be a catch. The umpire raised

---

[17] Opted to stop batting rather than being dismissed. This is done when a batting side feels they have enough runs on the board, or time is against them.

his finger; the batsman walked, sure that he was out. He was almost back to the pavilion when I sidled over to the captain. "Henley, the ball bounce, you know," I said. "What?" asked Henley, incredulous. "The ball touch the ground," I repeated. The umpire was alerted, and the batsman called back to resume his knock. We still went on to win the championship.

At the school assembly, prizes were distributed. To the best batsman, a bat. For the pick of the bowlers, another award. Then the principal announced a special prize for sporting conduct. I thought my head was going to burst as I walked up to receive a pair of batting gloves as my schoolmates cheered lustily. "That's what a QRC boy is all about," said the principal over the microphone as I accepted the prize. Me, the boy from 5 Remove—a class of boys who hadn't done well enough to move up to Form 6. The teachers treated me differently after that. I'd earned their respect by telling the truth. The bump ball affair made me somebody in QRC.

There was no doubt, in my second and final year at Queen's Royal College in 1960, that our football team was 50% better than the championship-winning team from the year before. Hinkson had moved on, and I was between the uprights. Once again, we met St Mary's in the final, but their team was severely depleted and we were certain of victory. It was just a matter of showing up and giving them four. In the first half, we scored three. The ref called back every one.

In the second, the Saints had one of their few shots of the game. Horton, a powerful kicker, got loose and hit one across the goal. I parried it, and the ball fell in front of my open goal, waiting for a bandy-legged Saints player to bumble along and tap it in. We had lost 1-0. After the match, we sat in silence, attempting to digest a corn cob.

"Abe, we really lose in truth?" asked my teammate Deryck Murray. "Tell me I dreaming."

Where it all started—
my Mom, Anita.

The gateway to my hometown, St James.

The Black Panther (in black) and my first youth team, Spatak.

Carlton "Carlie" Dore
—mentor.

Albert "Pa" Aleong
—mentor and football guru.

My alma mater, Queen's Royal College.

QRC cricket team, Inter-collegiate champions 1959 and 60.
(Back Row): Lincoln Phillips, Brian Murray, Royce Moore,
Glenroy Miller, Gary Dore, Ian Jones, Garvin DeSilva, Victor Gamaldo
(Front Row): Ellery Jones, T.V. Haynes (Principal), Anthony
Cuthbert (captain), Deryck Murray, Billy Samuel

(Back Row): Johnny Perriera, Ian Jones (captain),
Winty Samuel, Kenny Nasib, Billy Samuel.
(Center Row): Deryck Murray, Lincoln Phillips, Victor Gamaldo
(Front Row): Hubert Gamaldo, McGregor Hinkson, Tony Campbell

Coming off my line to intercept a through-
ball. Defender Rawle Boland follows up.

4—BUILDING A MONSTER

Washington, DC
1970

Ted Chambers knew nothing about football. Hold up! Hold up! You'll say I maligned the man; a man who gave me a job that took me to heights I could never have imagined. Alright, let me start over: Ted Chambers was an African-American physical education instructor at Howard University, a historically-black university in Washington DC. He knew very little about the sport Americans refer to as soccer.

You can ask anyone who knew him.

Chambers was the figurehead coach of the Howard Bisons soccer team. While he carried the title of "Coach," he acted more like a manager, leaving tactics and training in the hands of the team captain (who often abused his position by picking his friends to play). Howard recruited heavily from the African diasporas outside the United States, and Chambers had introduced soccer and cricket to ease the transition to North America for Caribbean and African students.

He was an approachable man who genuinely cared about his athletes. If the soccer team was going to New York, Chambers always dispensed the allowance—$25 for each traveling player. Many a thrifty man returned with that $25 still in his pocket.

While Chambers didn't know the finer details of the world's most popular sport, he did know something about racial prejudice. He'd been raised in the South and felt the sting of segregation laws through much of his life. As a youngster, he learnt what it was like to peep through a fence at pairs of white legs pursuing a ball, and how it felt to arrive thirsty at a water fountain to read the dreadful words: **Whites Only**. In the late 1960s, he traveled by bus with the soccer team to an away game. The men stopped to eat at a roadside rest-stop and were turned away. Chambers got back on the bus and cried.

This was the man who spotted me at a soccer clinic for the physically challenged at the University of Maryland in 1970. After recognizing me as keeper/coach of the semi-pro Washington Darts, several young men had requested a demonstration. I was tired, but obliged. The boys were getting a kick out of seeing me trap and shoot, and started throwing balls for me to head. As Chambers told it, he was on his way to his car when he heard cheering and looked over his shoulder to see a small group clapping and urging a man dressed all-in-black to keep on heading balls that were being slung his way.

The game became more fun for them as they threw the ball further away from my body, forcing me to stretch to get it. Eventually I got one that I couldn't head with any power, so I brought it under control with my noggin, and volleyed it into the goal. Chambers was watching closely. He asked where I was from and said he'd only seen one other person head with such power—my countryman, Noel Carr, who had played for Howard in the 1960s. He didn't have to ask twice about having me do some guest coaching at the most prestigious black college in the United States.

I've been consistent in one thing throughout my career: I've always been a hard taskmaster. So it had been with the Trinidad and Tobago Regiment team, and so it was when I coached (and played for) the Washington Darts.

The Darts were a hot team. The whole forward line was quick, and I wasn't bad in net myself. My name appeared in the Guinness Book of Records in 1969 for most consecutive soccer games without giving up a goal. Twelve matches I went without having to retrieve the onion from the back of the old onion bag. That year, we won the championship. The team was stocked with Trinidadians who had played on the T&T national team, including Victor Gamaldo, the man who married my wife's sister.

The camaraderie at the Darts was good; sometimes too good. One afternoon at an unusually desultory practice in Washington, the boys snickered and joked as I put them through their paces. On the 45-minute drive back to Baltimore (five of us Trinis lived together at the time), no one said a word as I silently seethed. "Put on your cleats," I said as we walked through the front door. "We going to practice."

Gamaldo pleaded that his knee was hurt. "You gonna punish five guys for a whole team that didn't practice well!" he scoffed. Poor fella; he grumbled all the way to the nearest playing field.

My tenure with the Darts lasted three seasons, until we lost the 1970 championship and feisty Scottish manager Norman Sutherland decided that he wanted to keep me on as goalkeeper while bringing in a new coach. This meant cutting my salary. Knowing I was the best keeper in the league, I said I'd only continue playing if Sutherland kept paying me as a player-coach. I needed the entire income to keep going to school to get my Physical Education degree. But Sutherland wouldn't back down.

Life in the United States was hard enough already. My two boys were still in Trinidad and Linda pined for them terribly. My immigration status was contingent on being employed as a soccer player, so we lived just one torn ligament away from having to make our way back home. But it was in the U.S. that I'd have the chance to play, coach, and get an education. And besides, I'd already endured Gamaldo's stewed chicken, wrestled two hardback[18] men for the warmth of a lint-covered bedspread named Fuzzy Wuzzy (at the home of friends who kindly accommodated three imported soccer players on weekends), and found myself knee deep in slop at a dye factory. How much worse could it get?

The conflict with Sutherland haunted me beyond the playing field. When I went to check on the status of my residency, the counter clerk showed me a list of names put forward by the Darts manager. I scanned it in disbelief. All the Trinidadians I'd recruited for the team and brought to the United States were on it: Victor Gamaldo, Gerry Brown, Bertram Grell. And there were the names of my English teammates. No Lincoln Abraham Phillips. In front of the clerk, I began to cry.

"Forget Norman Sutherland," she said calmly. "Let's go through the Recreation Department." She knew I'd been hosting soccer clinics for the District of Columbia's recreation division, and advised the director of the program to write a few letters saying that he couldn't find anyone to do the job because no one around knew a lick about the sport. It worked. That kind woman was just one in a succession

---

18 Adult.

of people who have shown the way when I've encountered seemingly insurmountable barriers. Her name was Cristina Jorgensen. I call her an angel. With my residency taken care of, I made a stand I'm still proud of: I went to Sutherland and quit the team.

The Darts and I were done for. Along comes Ted Chambers, his tonsured head gleaming in the sun as he crosses the Howard University sports field. He has found an Ethiopian by the name of Dr. Salah Yousif to coach the team while he manages. There are a few quality players on the squad, but the majority are mediocre.

This is a black college team in a country where soccer is just moving out of the immigrant communities. Most of the players are West Indians (with a heavy emphasis on Trinidadians) and Africans. There's not a single American on the side. It's a .500 team in 1969, meaning that they lose just as many as they win. At that first Howard clinic, I had everybody moving like greased lightning. Regimental discipline—just as we'd had at the army barracks in Chaguaramas, Trinidad. And total emphasis on fitness. You never know what you can do until you're fit enough to do it.

After the clinic, a slim defender who had played for Malvern in Trinidad's First Division came to me. "Coach want you bad," said Rick Yallery-Arthur, referring to Chambers. "Come and see him." Chambers already had drawn up a contract. He signed me up for $2,000, less than I'd been making with the Darts.

I don't have to tell you that soccer was not top of the Howard University totem pole. Those fellas were playing games in baseball socks, and they had to wait for the American football team to finish practicing on the school's single multi-purpose field before they could even sniff a ball. The sports hierarchy was laid down by athletic director Leo Miles, whose stocky frame could be seen swaggering around the sports fields. Miles is a footballer through and through. He played quarterback for his championship-winning DC high school and was briefly a cornerback for the New York Giants of the NFL. Football is king, says Miles. Basketball is queen. Soccer must be a footman to the prince.

Apart from my new position coaching the soccer team, I needed to get into Howard to complete my Physical Education degree. The school agreed to accept my credits from the other institutions I'd attended. Even better, they waived my tuition in exchange for teaching the Phys Ed department's soccer class. That wasn't a problem. It was a problem, however, to teach archery.

The class was oversubscribed, and I was called upon with just enough time to attend a couple classes and read the manual. When a female archer couldn't get close to the target, I picked up a bow to demonstrate. TWINGGGG! The whole class hooted as the arrow sailed past the coloured circles. "This bow is defective," I announced, picking up another. "Lord, please let me hit this," I prayed. TWANGGG! Straight in the bull's eye. "The problem was the bow," I announced. "It was not strung properly."

We had our fun, but Howard was not a frivolous place. It was a university alright, with all that label implies—sexually charged youth, late-night parties, an easily calculable ratio of incorrigible class-skippers—but the atmosphere at the school in the late 60s was shaped by the Civil Rights movement. Black people demanded their due, and a large portion of the student body was acutely focused on politics and race. Giant 'fros bobbed through public spaces. (Your hair, of course, said everything about your political sympathies.) The student body barricaded campus gates with desks and trashcans, demanding that the administration implement a Black Studies program. (One of my players insists that he saw some students trying to electrify a fence during an attempt to shut down the school.) In every room, black icons were pictured: guitarist Jimi Hendrix, or sprinters Tommie Smith and John Carlos—famous for their black-gloved salute at the 1968 Olympics.

Civil Rights leaders electrified the campus with their visits. Pan-Africanist Stokely Carmichael, who happened to be Trinidadian and a Howard graduate, easily pulled 3,000 to a talk in the gym. In the 60s, he was often seen on campus, recruiting for the Freedom Riders, who were risking arrest and beatings by riding segregated buses into the South. Angela Davis, imprisoned on racist charges for murder and kidnapping, was named Homecoming Queen even as she languished in prison. "Free Angela" stickers plastered the campus, and women grew proud Naturals[19] because of her. Soon after she was acquitted, Davis made her way to campus to speak.

---

[19] Unstraightened hairstyles—Afro or otherwise.

By the 70s when I arrived, the atmosphere had mellowed, but civil rights was still very much in the air. And you might still see Carmichael, sitting by the library, deep in conversation. Each player on the soccer team had to decide what the struggle meant to him.

I was a Caribbean boy from a majority black country that had recently been turned over to a black government; the depth and scale of America's history of racial injustice was still sinking in. Howard clarified things for me. I was never militant, but I was certainly aware. We needed to let people know that coloured people were the best at everything we did. Black talent had to be number one.

In 1970, I had the bones of a decent team, and badly wanted to turn those bones into a fearsome specimen that never tired. I began my effort back at home. I had stocked the Darts with my countrymen; I decided I would do the same to build the Howard Bisons.

Each time I spent my Christmas vacation in Trinidad, Catholic priest Father Reginald De Four invited me to run a soccer camp at St Mary's College. There, I spotted a diminutive forward with a short burst of speed who could shoot accurately with both feet. He was effective in the air despite his height, and he always found himself in the right place to score goals. He had helped his school to the national college title in 1968. Alvin Henderson was Pick #1 of my Howard career.

Alvin had plans to study medicine in England. "Listen man, we have one of the best medicine schools in the country," I said. "If you come to Howard, you won't pay any money *and* you'll play football." Before this, the school had never given out soccer scholarships. (They wouldn't have had a clue who they should give them to.) Alvin took the bait.

Coach Chambers came with me to Trinidad, too. Not to be outdone, he snuck off to make a pick of his own. I did not learn until we returned to Washington DC that another Trinidadian had been given a scholarship. Chambers found Trevor Mitchell in the Diego Martin League playing for a team called Sinfin. Trevor was never a starter, but did score a divinely inspired goal off the bench one day that led me to rechristen him "Spirit". He has never been able to shake the name.

My next bit of good fortune came in the form of a man who was part blessing. Keith Aqui was lean and lightning fast, with a Hendrixian head of hair. He had come to Howard to study psychology, heard there was a soccer team, and decided to check out a practice. He was a hard drinking, cigarette-smoking older student who had played extensively at club level in Trinidad and claims he wasn't very impressed with that first session because the ball was being beaten back and forth. Yet he stuck around.

The guy was opinionated, and Gawd, he could grumble. But he could also play. Having such a fast player gives a coach latitude to do a lot of different things. I had Keith run diagonally towards the space behind a defence, which prised teams open like cans of sardines. He was stubborn at times, while Alvin was the most coachable player I ever had. Together, they embarrassed lesser teams with nets full of goals and turned into one of the deadliest striking combinations ever to play NCAA soccer. After Alvin passed Keith a ball, he had to break his neck to get to the box before the ball came sizzling across from Keith's boot on the wing. Both went on to play professionally on the same team as I did.

Huddled together before our first match in 1970, I announced that I had a prayer. "That's my man!" enthused Chambers. "The prayer is not to win," I said. "It's to go out there and not get hurt, and not hurt anybody." Then I said the 121st Psalm, which my mother had taught me to strengthen me for life in this world. "The Lord shall preserve thy going out and thy coming in," I ended. "From this time forth, and even for evermore." Then Chambers said his own prayer. "Lord, help us to win, but if we lose, help us not to cry over spilt milk or lose the lesson." It was a less politically correct time back then; no one complained about partaking in Christian prayers before matches. And I think they all got the message: Don't be afraid.

They weren't. The win-one-lose-one Bisons from the previous season had disappeared. We steamrolled to the quarter-finals against Philadelphia University, better known as Philadelphia Textile. And that's where everything tun ol' mas.[20]

It was an away game for us, at Philadelphia, a team that boasted a couple rough-and-tumble Bermudans. One in particular liked to punch on the sly. Given the chance, he'd gladly extend a neck-high clothesline. Much of the time, there was no referee's whistle as they booted my guys around. At half-time, I told the ref to get it under control. When he didn't, I sent on Jamaican Mike Tomlinson,

---

[20] Descended into farce.

better known as "Savage." "Yeeeessss, Coach!" affirmed the bench. Savage, who really was a brute of a man with obscenely thick calves, immediately put down a flying tackle, straight at an opponent's thighs.

On this day, poor 5' 7", 17-year-old Alvin Henderson, a pacifist by nature, was getting the worst of it. The Bermudan kicked him across his waist, and as he was going down, Alvin uncharacteristically attempted to strike. He did not connect, but this was the signal for mass chaos.

The packed stands, including a band of vocal and intoxicated traveling Caribbean fans, emptied onto the field. In one corner, a former Howard player by the name of Oswyn Rose punched a guy until he staggered like a drunk. Rose then circled the pitch and drop-kicked an old fellow. In another corner, Howard goalkeeper Billy Jones grabbed an opposing player and sank his teeth into him. I tried to remove him, but it felt like someone had cast a piece of iron in concrete and let it set for too long before changing his mind. In the midst of the mêlée, Keith Aqui sucked an orange slice. The next thing I saw was twenty of the biggest policemen ever produced, hustling onto the field. Rose was in danger of being captured by the dispensers of justice, so I quickly pushed him into our retreating group. The giants escorted us out of town.

I got high marks for the handling of the incident from our vice-president of student affairs, Dr. Carl Anderson, but the match still had to be replayed. The National Collegiate Athletic Association (NCAA) decided it would be played on the same ground, without spectators. The stands were empty, but the Philadelphia fans pressed tight against the chain link fence surrounding the field. The new ref was a short bald guy who looked like tough 1970s TV cop Kojak. His name was Harry Newak. Newak read the Riot Act to the captains before play began. "All yuh doh touch nobody today," our captain, Bermudan Stan Smith reported. "He eh making joke." Players picked up their opponents after tackling them that day. Some even dusted off their adversaries' shorts. Someone chirped early on and Newak bawled: "SHADDDAAAAP!" Three fouls were committed for the entire match. We won 1-0.

In the semis, I had the first real challenge of my Howard coaching career: Who to put in net? Billy Jones from Sierra Leone was in his final year at the university and had started most of the season in goal.

But in the rematch against Philadelphia, it didn't take long to see that he'd lost his mojo. Some players say a headfirst encounter with the post while making a save had rattled him; others argue that he was shaken by the brawl. In the Philadelphia replay, I'd pulled him off in favour of our junior Nigerian keeper, the rangy Adelajah. A shot flew towards the corner of our net, and suddenly, there were Adelajah's hands pulling it down. The boy saved brilliantly to take us to the semi.

Before the semi-final, a couple senior players lobbied for Billy to start. The guy walked with a knife. Once, on DC's mean streets, he'd stabbed a mugger repeatedly. I thought he might bounce back mentally from whatever was troubling him. On the other hand, Adelajah had played such a good game to get us where we were . . . In the end, I opted for Billy.

Against UCLA, we led 3-2 with fifteen minutes to play. Keith Aqui was ripping through the side, but Billy looked shaky and had already let one in through his legs. As UCLA drew even, Keith turned to the bench. "What you going to do about that?" he barked. I realized I had to pull my keeper, but I was paralyzed by thoughts of his seniority. Adelajah would have his chances in future. As UCLA stormed back to a 4-3 victory, I felt I had singlehandedly lost the game. The milk was spilt, and despite Chambers' admonition I was ready to cry.

By previous standards, however, the season had been a success. We ended with twelve victories, one loss and a draw, and returned to a press conference at the airport outside DC. "We are going to be sensational in 1971," crowed Chambers. Little Howard University, pride of Black America, had made it to an NCAA semi-final.

It was the best the school had ever done in team sports.

5—TIGER

Queen's Park Savannah, Trinidad 1960

"Tiger! RAAAAHHHR!" That's Maple football club supporter Guy Corbie urging me on from the sideline. The man is such a fan that he tries to instruct the Maple captain on who he should pick on any given day. He is such a fan that he gives me two sticks of gum for luck before each game. "Come on, man," he claps. "Tiiiger! Tiiiger!" What got into Corbie's head to suddenly call me Tiger, I'll never know. Maybe he recognized the goalkeeping lineage, coming down from the Black Panther, my boyhood hero, and decided to place me in the same family of big cats. Tiger. It stuck.

Like the Panther, I wore all black. And here I was starting for Maple. The team was not my first choice. In fact, Maple was the enemy. I had been 'Malvern to the bone' since boyhood. But at 19-years-old in 1960, just leaving Queen's Royal College and in need of a club to call home, my preferred team was out of the question. Standing between the posts, guarding the net and his job, was Clive Burnett, one of the best goalkeepers ever to play in the country. I was not about to compete with him. So when Maple called me for tryouts, I obliged.

Known as "The Government" because its players were mostly civil servants, Maple had struggled to find a regular keeper since the Panther had moved on. But now that I'd sunk my claws into the job, I wasn't letting go. The crowds in front of the Savannah grand stand were larger and more animated than any I'd played in front of before, even at Intercol finals against St Mary's College. Football was a national obsession. This was long before the steady stream of European football that cable TV provides today, and local first division footballers were supermen in their communities and on the pitch. It wasn't unusual to have a couple hundred spectators turn up at practice.

And talk 'bout bet! There was a side of fellas who gambled on everything. Our captain Sedley Joseph found it strange before a match at the Oval one afternoon when defender Ronald Woods trotted past him just as Sedley was leading the team onto the grass over the concrete cycle track. Sedley always ran out first. "I tell a man to bet that I would reach the grass before you," admitted Woods after the game.

The football clubs were divided by class and race. Malvern was working class, Shamrock and Casuals were the local white boys and the fairer-skinned graduates of prestige secondary schools, and Maple was non-white and educated. We all gravitated to where we felt comfortable. When we met, we clashed hard and shook hands afterward. On the national team, there were black players and white players, but no discrimination.

Under Sedley, an even-tempered employee of the Customs and Excise Division who everyone respected as captain, Maple won the league shield three years in a row. During that time, I had a string of twenty shutouts, due in large part to the resolute defence in front of me. But even great defenders have bad days. (So do great keepers.) Playing the young upstarts, Dynamo, we dominated but couldn't score. On a harmless shot by a Dynamo forward, national player Tyrone "Tank" De La Bastide, went up to head it away. I had the ball covered until it skidded off Tyrone's head and into my goal. As fortune would have it, a *Guardian* photographer got a good shot of me in no-man's land, grimacing as the treacherous sphere sailed past. We made Dynamo defend with ten men after that, but lost—one deflected goal to nil. The *Guardian* published the photograph with the caption "That same one . . ." It was a popular Brook Benton song about a lover begging his fickle woman to come back.

At the time, I worked at The Sports Centre, owned by Robert Farrell and managed by Carlton Dore, who everyone knew as "Carlie." The morning after the game, Carlie went to the *Guardian* early and got a copy of the picture, which he generously enlarged before pasting it up in the store window. Each time the schoolboys passed that day—on the way to school, on the way to lunch, on the way back from lunch, and on the way home—they pranced in front of the door, pointing and chanting: "One in your ass! One! One in your ass! One!" Four times I endured it: "One in your ass, one!" I felt I could run into the street and strangle a schoolboy while the others scampered for their lives, but I respected Carlie too much to reveal my mood. I bit my tongue. My blood boiled. The last time the rascals passed, Carlie said: "I really admire you. I like how you handled them. Those are your fans." Not since the QRC principal had hoisted me up as a role model had I felt my head tingle and hair stand on end.

In my youth, I was not particularly good at defeat. Victory I enjoyed. Defeat made me drag for days. Sitting on her tiny verandah in Diego Martin, where we lived for a while, my mother always knew whether I'd won or lost from the time she laid eyes on me. Shuffling along, head bowed, I must have looked a pitiful sight. She cooed to me while taking off my shoes. "Don't worry about that. Next time. You hadda train harder. You can't always play well." The sound of her voice ate away at the lump of distress lodged in my chest.

My mother was an Anglican from a family of Jehovah's Witnesses, and I grew up in a God-fearing environment. On Sundays, I attended mass at St Mary's Roman Catholic Church. Then, from the age of nine, I added religious instruction at St Crispin's English Catholic to my devotional schedule. (All this lasted until football and cricket consumed the Sabbath too.) So when my mother handed me a worn prayer book and directed me to the 121st Psalm, she was sowing a seed in fertile ground. It became the prayer I would return to throughout my life. "The sun shall not smite thee by day, nor the moon by night," it reads. "The Lord shall preserve thee from all evil. He shall preserve thy soul."

Somehow, it helped me understand winning and losing. Sometimes you win, sometimes you lose, but I felt that God was always with me, and if I lost, it was for a reason. My players came to know the psalm as part of my pre-match ritual. When I skipped it before a big game at Howard University one day, the omission was noticeable. "Coach, you forget the prayer," said a player.

I said the psalm helped; I didn't say that it sealed my tear ducts. Listen, I've always been a crier. Not a sob-if-a-man-bus'-my-head-with-a-big-stone type of crier, mind you; I'm only prone to lachrymation in the face of strong emotion. Two things have been known to open the floodgates: my family, and a tough loss.

In my first year at Maple, we lost 1-0 to our arch-rival Malvern in a big game—an FA Cup North Zone final. Fans of every stripe packed the stands and competing rhythm sections raised an almighty din. Malvern earned a throw about ten yards from our corner flag. Everyone could see when they took it that it was a foul throw.[21] It just looked sloppy. Malvern forward Carlton Franco trapped the ball, but turned away from it as a whistle blew. Everyone relaxed. Suddenly, Franco turned back to the ball and booted it into the area for Kelvin Berassa to head and score. I was confused. As Franco walked away from me, I asked what had happened. "The ref said, 'Play ball,'" he answered. "It wasn't his whistle." The goal stood.

Back at the clubhouse on Ariapita Avenue, our fans were doing what losing fans do: drinking, grumbling, and making excuses. "Boy, this is robbery," went the refrain. We'd gone twenty consecutive games without giving up a goal, only to lose like this. I was standing at the corner waiting on a taxi when captain Sedley Joseph and teammate Conrad Braithwaite went by in a car. I must have looked pathetic. "Tiger!" they yelled simultaneously. As I opened my mouth to respond, I began to bawl. I was 19-years-old, man. I sobbed as they drove me home. "Jesus Christ," said the driver. "I never know anybody could take a game so hard." When a few teammates came looking for me next morning, my eyes were swollen big.

The newspaper ran an op-ed; it said that a stupid person with a whistle had decided the match.

At the same time, the newly formed Trinidad and Tobago Regiment had a problem. Two truckloads of soldiers had descended on the fishing village of Carenage, hurling boulders and beating everyone in sight. Using batons, smoke bombs, knives, bottles and stones, the soldiers rampaged, injuring five including "a wayside Baptist preacher woman." It was not reported whether the apparent targets of the

---

[21] Called when the thrower raises a foot off the ground as he launches, or removes one of his hands from the ball prematurely.

attack, two fishermen who had allegedly stabbed a couple soldiers the week before, got their comeuppance, but the press coverage certainly put the army's top brass in a tricky spot.

The T&T Regiment had only been established a year earlier, at independence in 1962. Before that, Britain's Caribbean colonies had been protected by the West India Regiment, comprised of recruits from each of the islands. The fledgling, national army was still under intense public scrutiny by citizens who needed to understand its role in the newly independent state. Beating up preachers did not inspire confidence, and Trinis started to question why we even needed an army.

To counter the stink of a commission of enquiry set up to probe the Regiment's community relations, Brigadier Joffre Serrette, an avid sports fan, came up with a plan: Let's start an army football team. If anything could improve the Regiment's image, it was disciplined soldiers playing sports.

On my way to a movie, sporting a flat-top hairstyle and a pair of simple suede boots (we called them "jigger" boots back then), I looked sharp. Regiment reserve officer Roderick Yates paused from watering his garden. "Young man, you have a minute?" Not really, no, I began, but Yates was polite and so was I. I stopped to hear him out. The man didn't get right to the point; he beat around a bit, asking what I saw myself doing in a few years. Was I just a player, or could I see myself commanding games on the field? (The answer to that one was obvious: I'd recently gained enough confidence to start instructing the Maple defenders, all of them a good bit older than me.) Yates had been feeding me; he was ready to set the hook. "Have you ever thought of joining the Regiment?" he asked. I jumped. Me! With all those hooligans! "I have to talk to Dad," I said. Clever fellow—I knew my father would never let me join that band of thugs.

Yates forged on. The Regiment, he said, is starting a number of teams—football, basketball, cricket, field hockey. We'd send you to England to study physical training. You'd instruct your fellow soldiers when you returned. I'll send someone by to see you and your father.

By then, I'd missed the show.

Lieutenant Dopwell glowed in his white dress-uniform. As he spoke about the opportunities I'd have in the military, my father nodded. He shocked the hell out of me after Dopwell left. "Join, boy, join," he said. I respected my father, but I knew sports didn't come first in the army. I was playing First Division football, already on the national basketball team, and on the verge of making the national football team, too. The military would destroy me as a sportsman.

I went to the entrance exam fully intending to fail. Obviously, I didn't do a very good job of it. They marked the exams immediately. I was given batch number 3085, and ordered to report to base the next day.

My flat-top was my pride and joy. "All you is saga boy,"[22] said the barber as he draped me in a plastic cape. "You in the army now." His clippers buzzed. "Eh no saga boy in here." It hurt to my guts to look down and see my flat-top on the floor.

With a 23-pound machine gun on the table in front of me, and Sergeant Pat James standing over my shoulder, I was having my first lesson. "Try it on your own," said James. Take the Bren gun apart, put it back together, take it apart again. I had arrived at camp months before the other recruits, so Sergeant James, better known as "Kid," drilled me and a couple other early arrivals in the essentials of soldiering. He taught us to smother our boots in Kiwi polish, and use the edge of a hot iron to melt away the tiny bumps that covered our new footwear. Then we rubbed with wet cotton until they gleamed. We marched daily, and I could soon take that Bren Gun apart and put it back together blindfolded.

The Regiment had brought me in to play sports, and I played them all. (Be thankful for sporting seasons.) But there were times when cricket, basketball, and football overlapped. I woke at dawn for a five-mile march, played a football game in the afternoon, moved on to basketball at night, and returned to camp where I shone my boots, or oiled my rifle to avoid being punished for a speck of dust. In life, we all set priorities. My first was definitely not maintaining a perfect kit. Were it not for my batch mate Carl Alfonso (who went on to become Brigadier Carl Alfonso) I might still be at base doing pushups and marching under heavy load. Dying after a full day of physical exertion, I often opened my locker to see my brass buttons winking,

---

22   One who dresses to impress.

my belt buckle gleaming, and my shoes shining like dog's stones on a moonlight night. Alfonso had cleaned them all.

When the Land Rover dropped me at the governor-general's residence for a late-night, two-hour sentry shift, Alfonso was there again. He knew I'd trained for cricket that morning, before playing a football match and finally taking part in a basketball game at the Princes Building Grounds. As I struggled out of the jeep at the guard hut, Sergeant Byer, better known as "Corn Pone" by those who loved to hate him, growled. He has no compassion does Corn Pone. Alfonso, due to end his own shift and return to base, snapped to attention and offered to take my shift. Pone relented and sent me back to base. When he finally returned to camp, Alfonso found me fast asleep in my basketball uniform.

The Regiment plundered the best footballers in the country from the first division clubs. No other club could offer a player a job. I personally approached several national players and got them to commit to a stint with the armed forces. Kelvin Berassa, who'd made me cry when he scored for Malvern after the spectator's whistle, was one of them. Victor Gamaldo would soon earn his first national cap. He joined up, too. Clive Niles, Philbert Prince, Gerry Brown, Tony Inniss, Benito Sambrano, Dennis Thomas—footballing and cricketing acquaintances all—were snared by the Regiment net.

As player-coach of the football team, I was responsible for training all the sporting recruits. Dressed in my tracksuit, I worked them hard, and some of them resented me. For two years, we struggled in the first division football league, but by 1965 we were champions. The year was a good one for me. At the annual West Indian Tobacco sports awards, I was voted player of the year in both basketball and football.

I was not the perfect soldier. I didn't enjoy long training exercises in the bush, and my arm was crooked when I marched. (You've never seen a soldier stand as straight as Carl Alfonso, who was great at offering advice to new recruits, but challenged when it came to marriage counseling. His first marriage was to my sister, Marilyn; he kept trying after that.) Unlike Alfonso, I was not fastidious. But I was disciplined, and a leader on the playing field. After nine weeks of training by English officers, Alfonso and I each got our first stripe. Lance corporal Lincoln Phillips, if you please. I went on to become a corporal, and later earned the rank of sergeant. I was the first in my batch of recruits to get those three stripes.

The army was the centre of my life, but I had a girlfriend to see when I wasn't on duty. Sprucing up to meet her, I'd walk into the bathroom with my towel over my shoulder, whistling all the way. Since I didn't always remember to buy toiletries, I'd sidle up to a soldier as he was about to brush his teeth, and swipe the toothpaste off his brush. Quick as a wink, I popped my brush into my mouth. Bubbles were forming before the soldier could react. I wore black off the field as well as on it, and my footwear was always a pair of black Clarks jigger boots. After the trauma of my first barber shop visit, we were allowed to grow our hair, within limits. Alfonso will tell you that I got my flat-top just right by patting it down with a couple mess tins.[23] I certainly wasn't alone.

Linda D'andrade's father wasn't keen on me. Maybe it was the jigger boots and the flat-top. Maybe my skin was too dark for his fair-skinned girl who had Portuguese and Chinese blood in her veins. Maybe he was just an overprotective fellow who loved his daughters. Whatever it was, the man whistled for play to stop and it stopped.

Three years on, I was walking past the Oval when I saw Linda again. As she hopped off her bicycle, I mumbled: "Lincoln, you are a real ass in truth." Between the ages of 15 and 18, certain anatomical changes had taken place. They were all for the good. "We should get back together," I said, as I walked her home to Belmont. She replied that she'd never left. When she consulted with Ernest D'andrade, he reluctantly agreed. I was on the verge of joining the army; play could resume.

It was Ernest's absence that had given me the chance to get close to my future wife in the first place. He was out of the country when Linda asked her mother to go out on the streets of St James on Carnival Tuesday night. (She was a maverick compared to her sisters. Choosing a musical instrument, she opted for the steelpan over piano or guitar. Pan, at the time, was the music of the seething rabble.) I was jumping up in the band like a warrior when I saw pretty, sheltered Linda D'andrade, who lived just down the road, moving through the crowd. Smooth as silk, she put her arms around my waist and we

---

[23] Portable saucepans.

chipped along to the music. By the time we parted, our relationship had begun.

On April 18, 1965, I put on my brilliant white army dress-uniform with the green trim and gold braid, and went to the Holy Rosary Church. It was a rainy Easter Sunday and I was nervous as hell. "What if she jilts me?" I wondered after standing at the altar for 45 minutes. "The army boys would kill me." The story would be all over the press! An hour late, Linda walked up the aisle looking as lovely as I could have imagined. She'd been delayed by a tardy flower delivery. Here was my wife; future mother of four sons.

No doubt about it—Pat Gomez was getting long in the tooth. Not that the man hadn't been good! I remember watching him train when I was young. He could dive, and moved like a cat. But by the time I was maturing as a keeper in 1963, the captain of the national team wasn't judging the ball as well as he once had. I was picked as his backup for a three match tour to Suriname.

Sitting on the bench, I watched Gomez give up a couple soft goals from the wings as we lost 3-1. Delighted? Let's just say I wasn't heartbroken. After the match, the players, led by my captain at Maple, Sedley Joseph, approached manager Noel Pouchet and lobbied for my inclusion. "How can I cut the team captain?" asked Pouchet. Obviously, he figured it out. That same afternoon, he did the necessary. I was in. Gomez was out. He went to teammate Henry Govia and asked what Govia would do if he were in his shoes. "Boy, I wouldn't like to be in your shoes," he answered.

In my first game for the national team, I found out just how good the Surinamese were. They strung together short, crisp passes in a style similar to the South Americans, and wing-back August Wooter could bend a ball like Beckham. Ours was a simpler style, but we held our own and leveled the series with a 2-1 win. It was my first win in national colours.

In the third and final match, I was bombarded. In my arrogance, I'd always believed that no one could score on me from outside the area. The Surinamese were out to prove me wrong. But Jesus, I was on fire! Leaping everywhere, and catching balls single-handed. I went flying for one that curved away from me and found loving embrace in the back of the net. Another blast, I pushed into the woodwork. It hit me in the back of the head and scored. I have no idea how many I saved, but I do know that four got through. It's there on the scorecard for all to see: Suriname—4, T&T—3.

Despite the 2-1 series loss, the team was in good spirits when we touched down at Piarco International Airport. We crossed the tarmac shoulder-to-shoulder, singing that year's Road March-winning calypso, Kitchener's "The Road Make to Walk." We had narrowed the gap with an opponent who had beat up on our national teams in the past. "We lost the series," said the magnanimous captain whose reign as national keeper had ended, "but we really played wonderful football. That final match could have gone either way." Team manager Pouchet singled me out for praise, telling the *Guardian* that the Surinamese crowds thought I was the finest goalie they had seen in many years.

Two years later, at the Queen's Park Oval, I faced the Surinamese again, in T&T's first-ever World Cup qualifying match. This time, watched by a hometown crowd of 10,000, we got the better of our South American nemesis, 4-1. We didn't qualify for the World Cup, but my best tournament for T&T was yet to come.

No one thought we'd make it out of the group stage of the Pan-American Games in 1967. The T&T Football Association was so sure we'd be trounced by formidable Latin American opponents Argentina, Colombia, and Mexico, that they booked our tickets to leave the quadrennial games, held that year in Winnipeg, Canada, for the day after our final group match. Such "confidence" called for a response.

First up was Colombia, who we beat with the spirited backing of a small T&T crowd that chanted lustily and banged out a rhythm on iron percussion. The players also loved music and before the match against Mexico, a team that had played to draws with France and Uruguay in the World Cup in England the year before, we began to sing: "Run your run, Mexico run your run/ Run your run, Mexico run your run/ If you hear what Trinidad say/ With a piece of rope and a mango tree, we go hang up you goalie." I handled a barrage of shots against the Mexicans and we eked out a draw. Then, miraculously, we put one on Argentina and shut the shop door tight. We had qualified for the semi-finals at the top of our group. There was a mad scramble to change our tickets home.

Three very good teams had been well-handled. Now only tiny Bermuda, smaller and less populous than even T&T, stood in the way of the gold medal match. The singing reached new heights. Sparrow's "Gunslingers" seemed appropriate: "We young and strong, we eh fraid a soul in town!/ They think they bad, to beat them we more than glad/ We got we guns and we eh making fun/ If you smart, clear the way/ If you think you bad, make you play."

The practice before the semi was lethargic. Jovial players jogged through the skills. "Hmmm, it look like we win this silver medal already, boy," remarked the ever sober Sedley Joseph. We encountered the Bermudans at breakfast on the day of the match and gave them a little fatigue[24] about the fruit their coach had them eating. "All yuh could eat what all yuh want," remarked one of my pumped-up teammates. "We beating you all this evening."

I think you may already know what's coming . . .

We started the match like a hot knife carving through Bermudan butter. Our skilful left wing Alvin Corneal missed an easy one in the first seven minutes, and twice rattled the woodwork. Their keeper let one through his legs, but managed to turn around and snuffle it up. Then, things turned Bermuda's way. Clyde Best, who went on to become one of the first black players to play in the English first division, fell outside our area, but managed to get back up. BADANG! That's the ball rebounding off a backstop directly behind the goal. Best had booted it with unimaginable ferocity, and it had passed me in a blur. Before we knew it, Bermuda was up 2-0. Now, we buckled down and started to play. We managed to pull one back. That would be all we got.

We crawled into the bus and propped our heads on our hands. I heard singing, way off in the distance. As it got a little closer, I realized it was Bermuda. "Run your run! Trinidad, run your run!" They rocked the bus and sang, with us sitting disconsolate inside. When they finally left us alone, we raised our heads. In a lilting voice, one man began to sing: "Oh, dearrr, what can the matter be?" Everyone joined in. In the bronze medal match, we beat the hosts Canada four goals to nil. That bronze remains the only medal ever won by a T&T football team at the hemispheric Pan Am Games.

---

[24] Ribbing.

Sports psychology has since clarified the lesson of that tournament for me. There are three timeframes—past, future, and present. If you're thinking about the last game, which you played so well, you're going to lose. If you start thinking about how you're going to celebrate the gold, you're going to mess up the present. It's called divided focus. I was party to it when QRC lost against St Mary's in the college final of 1960, and again at the Pan Games. I sincerely hoped never to contribute to it again.

The year we were married, Linda got pregnant. She was a few months along when the army lived up to its word and sent me off to England for Physical Training Instruction (PTI)—the expectation being that I would improve the fitness of the entire battalion when I returned. Man, she looked so beautiful when she saw me off, even with tears rolling down her face.

I arrived in mighty England as a corporal in January 1966, in the company of Private George Simon. We explored the metropolis together, awestruck by its modern conveniences. An escalator blew my mind, and when the door of a department store opened on its own, Simon made me go back outside to try it again. He looked at the closest store attendant quizzically, and asked: "You see the man raise his hand?"

Captain Desmond Whiskey of the T&T Regiment had been attending officer training school, so he introduced us to public transit and showed us around. When Whiskey left for home, we saw him off at Waterloo Station, and I turned to Simon dejectedly. It was like our mother had left us. I returned to Earl's Court, where I was staying while training at Aldershot, and bumbled out of a station exit that I hadn't used before. Around and around I walked in the cold drizzle, missing my wife and my home. The sameness of the city threatened to choke me. Hopelessly lost, I stopped and lowered my head. When I raised it again, the sign of my lodging was hanging directly above me.

Simon was sent to a separate PTI course, while I spent my time at Aldershot in the company of thirty PTI trainees, the overwhelming majority of them British soldiers. Some of them were weird! One would sit at the dinner table and make a show of biting into a glass. "This" CRUNCH "tastes" CRUNCH "really good."

We were taught gymnastics (where I dislocated my nose) and scrambled up ropes (where my arms turned to rubber). Boxing against

Lt/Cpl J. Brannan, I danced around as the instructor yelled: "Guard! Guard!" Brannan belted me with a right, straight through my pathetic defence. I saw stars, I saw planets, the world turned green. Birds began to sing.

On the soccer pitch, I endured an embarrassing put-down by an instructor who was handing out the gear. "In your country," he asked, "do you wear boots?" The sergeant major roared at the poor chap for his willful ignorance, before I humbled their countrymen on the field. At basketball, I played dead to catch corbeaux alive.[25] I was already playing for Trinidad and Tobago's national basketball team, but pretended to take the basic dribbling skills very seriously. When the instructors matched up against the best of the students, I drove to the hoop, jumped, faked right, then left, and laid up for a basket. "You made an ass of me!" complained an instructor who'd been thoroughly convinced that I was a basketball novice.

In April 1966, I earned my Physical Training certificate. My report card said: "Corporal Phillips is a very enthusiastic student who has the ability to develop into a first class unit PT instructor." Thanks to the training, I was fitter and stronger than I'd ever been. I was also entitled to wear the insignia of the crossed swords, reserved for army PTIs.

I'll admit, I used it to my advantage when I returned home. When they tried to send me out on guard duty, I said, "No no; PTIs don't go on guard." Dressed in a lily white vest with the crossed swords stamped on the front, white shorts, and white sneakers, I was also exempt from the dreaded Muster Parade, where you stood for hours in the sweltering sun.

Needless to say, higher-ranking soldiers didn't appreciate my perks. They became even more annoyed when I approached my superior and informed him that the sergeants were the most unfit men in the Regiment. They had been living it up in the mess hall—eating and drinking with abandon. Soon, I had them running at 0600. The least fit asked permission to fall out so they could vomit in the bushes. They huffed and puffed with logs hoisted overhead. Big fat Captain Mc Comie lost so much weight, he had to buy new clothes, and crowed that he felt like a new man.

---

[25] Feigned ineptitude to produce surprise—as a predator might fake death to catch a vulture, otherwise known as a *corbeau*.

At the Pan American military games, competing against armed forces from the region, our team was so confident of its superior fitness that they ran the entire march and shoot, which other teams usually completed by running twenty paces and marching twenty paces. The danger, if you ran, was that you'd be breathing so hard, you'd miss the targets. But by running, the T&T Regiment team got to the shooting range way ahead of the others, and lay down to catch their breaths. They shot down every single target and won the gold.

By now, Linda's belly was as swollen as a full zaboca.[26] I wanted to be a father so badly. On August 4, 1966, I found myself walking towards Park's Nursing Home with a mighty grin on my gob, singing to myself: "Boy, I have a son! A child!" Linda was lying in bed, and there was tiny Sheldon Lincoln Dominic Phillips all swaddled in a blanket. What an ugly little fella. One big mouth! When he cried, I thought his head was going to fall off. Of course, my initial impression was based on my utter ignorance of what a newborn looks like. Thankfully, the body grew around the mouth. Son, you're a good-looking chap today.

I was a sergeant now, and from time to time, I had to pull a little rank with my comrades, many of whom were equals on the field. After football practice one day, I hustled the players to change into their army uniforms to head out to the rifle range for grading. I gave them five minutes, but a few insubordinate players dragged their feet, causing us to leave late. When some soldiers flouted my order to double-march (run, basically) the group looked ragged, with some running and others strolling behind. "What the hell is going on!" yelled a senior officer who passed us in the opposite direction. I was mortified. I had no choice but to charge my own players with insubordination and disobeying a lawful command. Some were confined to barracks for twenty-one days.

They all stopped talking to me after that. My own friends and teammates wanted nothing to do with me. I had been forced, already, to forge some small distance between myself and my men. I couldn't

---

[26]   Almost-ripe avocado.

lime[27] or party with them as before. Doing so might have undermined my authority when moments like these arose.

Godfrey Achille, a solid central defender and the best basketball player in the country, led his fellow soldiers in expressing disgust at being disciplined. As captain of the Regiment basketball team, he had relished the opportunity to drop me after I returned from England with a heavy shooting hand, but put me back on the court when I'd regained my touch. He led the cabal of the discontented, but also healed the rift between me and my subordinates by singing loudly behind me at mess hall: "You've lost that loving feeling. And now it's gone, gone, gone . . . *Sergeant Phillips*." As I turned and laughed, the tension was broken.

I have always been both giver and receiver of nicknames. The first two I acquired from the silver screen. As teenagers in St James we were movie fans, and our cinema was *Rialto* at the corner of Agra Street and the Western Main Road. Now and then, we would step out and go to *Strand* or *Roxy*, but by and large, you could find us in Pit at *Rialto* where we paid 9 cents to sit on wooden chairs that broke up your backside. If, as occasionally happened, the film reel busted, plunging the theatre to black, an immediate uproar arose from the throats of the denizens of Pit, who heaped curses on the head of the man running the projector.

Wilfred Lewis, better known as "Cheesy," was one of the gang and behaved a lot like slapstick comedian Jerry Lewis, my favourite actor. On the way to a wedding one day, I dressed in a nice blue suit. It was checkered. A blue, checkered suit. I ran into Cheesy on the way to the wedding. "Where you going in that suit?" asked Cheesy. "You going to hunt tigers? You's *Harry Black?*" I'd paid nine cents to see *Harry Black* heading off to hunt a man-eating tiger in India; now, I'd assumed his name.

"Chief Crazy Horse" was a name I picked up on the basketball court. I was fast and athletic, hurling my body around and flying from pillar to post when I played for Regiment. Anywhere a ball was passed, I got to it. One night, I ran full tilt into the padded backboard support. The crowd gasped as I went down, and 'oohed' as I got up. The fearless, slightly crazy chief of the Lakota, who fought U.S. federal forces for

---

[27]   Hang out.

Indian territory had recently been fictionalized in a Hollywood film. It was only obvious that I be named after a wild Indian.

In St James and some small pockets of the army, I was Harry Black. On the basketball court, I was Chief Crazy Horse. And in the world of football, I was Tiger. Jesus Christ, Trinidadians like a name.

The Braves, my hometown basketball team.

Trinidad and Tobago national basketball team for the North,
Central American and Caribbean Games (Me, back right).

Take them knees! A big
crowd at a Maple game.

At full stretch for a high cross.

Sergeant Pat "Kid" James,
military mentor

Corporal Phillips, in full battle gear.

The Regiment football team, national club champions, with the
1965 Port of Spain Football League Shield. (I'm at left).

Physical Training—Aldershot, England.

The Trinidad & Tobago Regiment's first
basketball team—national champions.

Physical Training
Certificate

No. 85/66

AWARDED TO

No. 3085 RANK cpl

NAME PHILLIPS L A

ARM/SERVICE T + T R

BY THE
ARMY SCHOOL
OF
PHYSICAL TRAINING
ALDERSHOT

Marrying the lovely Linda D'Andrade at
the Rosary Church in Port of Spain.

"Well held, Sir!" was the caption on this photo in
the Trinidad Express. Corporal Bailey and Private
Guichard form the Regiment Honour Guard.

1965—The Trinidad and Tobago team before the country's
first ever World Cup qualifying match, against Suriname.

1966—After playing Mexico in Honduras, we
realized we could compete with the best.

CERTIFICATE OF AWARD

PRESENTED BY THE ORGANIZING COMMITTEE OF THE

V PAN-AMERICAN GAMES

JULY 22 TO AUGUST 7, 1967 · WINNIPEG, MANITOBA, CANADA

THIRD PLACE

TO

TRINIDAD & TOBAGO

IN

FOOTBALL

Lincoln A. Phillips

On the way to bronze at the Pan Am Games, we beat
Argentina, Colombia and Canada—then lost to Bermuda.

National Team: Pan American Games Bronze Medalists - 1967

Back Row - From Left: Conrad Brathwaite (Coach), Victor Gamaldo, Lincoln Phillips, Sedley Joseph, Hugh Mulzac, Jean Moutett, Governor Sir Solomon Hochoy, Jeff Gellineau, Bertrand Grell, Gerry Browne, Kelvin Berassa, Ivan Montes (Manager), Arnim David, Alvin Corneal
Front Row – From Left: Aldwyn Ferguson, Tyrone DeLabastide, Pat Small, Selwyn Murren, Richard Stewart

6—WE LIKE IT COLD

Howard University, Washington DC
1971

It was a cold, wet day in December. Playoffs were coming up and I had scheduled a practice for the Howard team. "Take off your sweatpants," I told the shivering group of West Indians and Africans. "Shorts only. If it cold, we like it cold. If it wet, we like it wet." They grumbled, but I had a duty to render these tropical specimens impervious to the weather. On days when other Howard teams huddled indoors, we went outside. It sent a message: who really wants to win?

Why did they follow me through the vomit-inducing hill runs and the frigid stretches? Maybe it was because I came with a no-nonsense army attitude. Perhaps they respected my national and professional soccer pedigree. Maybe they craved winning as much as I did.

I was no easy taskmaster. It was my way or the highway. Being an army sergeant, we don't *ask* you to do anything, we say: You are to do this. And if you don't, you are going to the brig. My players ran onto the pitch in a line, with stockings pulled up to their knees. They parted at the half-line in perfect sync—one goes left, the next goes right.

Mind you, there were challenges. This was the Afro era, but I liked my boys to keep their hair low. Everyone wore a bush as big as young Michael Jackson's. Chop them down, I ordered.

In 1972, Keith Look Loy arrived from St Mary's College in Trinidad. The boy was a good defender, but had a reputation as an independent thinker. The first thing you saw when Keith arrived was a giant 'fro.[28] It was tall, and it was wide, and he was very proud of it. All the players were just returning from summer break for the fall semester and the soccer season, so quite a few were unshorn. "Haircuts," I announced at the team meeting. "Have them done by next practice." The morning of the deadline, I picked up a little towel, a pair of scissors, and a comb, and shoved them into my bag.

The players were sitting outside the gym when I arrived. A few laughed as I approached. "What happened, Keith?" I asked. "You were supposed to get a haircut. Everybody else went and got their haircuts. They following rules. Playing football to win championships." He gave me a lame excuse, something like: The barber shop was closed. Keith was stubborn, but he wasn't stupid. When I told him to come into my office for a trim, he followed.

Now, I'm no barber. Each time I cut one side, it didn't match the other, so I kept moving from side to side trying to even it up. The shifting asymmetry was getting Keith hot. "Man, take it all off!" By the time I finished, he looked like a sheep shorn of its heavy woolen coat. He had a good few zogs[29] as well. When he walked out, the boys were waiting. Some flung themselves on the ground and writhed breathlessly; others ran around holding their bellies and bawling. They screamed and laughed until they cried. Keith was hurt and angry. "Before you command, you must comply," I said, in the hope that he would understand that he could lead one day. But I hadn't intended to cut it that low.

Keith lived in my house for his entire first semester at Howard. He had been called up at the last minute because another defender couldn't make it to school, and he hadn't been able to find a place to live on such short notice. I had promised his mother I'd look after her son. After the barbering fiasco, he devised a plan where he kept the front low and left the back long. The incident should have been fair warning. Keith Look Loy and I would eventually tangle over issues far more serious than hair.

There were social reasons for the haircuts: I knew the stigma attached to Afros in the 1970s. But I also liked my players to look neat. And I thought that Afros were not particularly helpful for heading. When Bermudan defender Stan Smith, who wet his hair down before games, jumped to head a ball from a corner kick, it went right through

---

[28]   Afro.

[29]   Hairdressing slips where the scalp is sometimes made visible.

his 'do and sat up for an opposition forward to hammer home. Understandably, I went on a rant.

Players had to sit out of championship photographs because they refused to cut their hair or beards! But, people change. In ten years at Howard, I gradually relaxed a few of my rules.

The softening began in the face of well-argued opposition from a dreadlocked Jamaican delegation. Mario Mc Lennan and Barnaby Tulloch—who I'd recruited after seeing them skip around the Howard team on a tour to Jamaica—both wore their dreads long. In my office, abundant tresses flowing from their heads, they quoted Old Testament verse and argued for religious exemption based upon a Rastafarian tenet: "They shall not make baldness upon their 'ead." (If you know Jamaicans, you'll know they don't pronounce the 'H' at the beginning of a word.) I said, "Fine, but you're playing for me now. I am the Lord here, and I make the decisions." They cut their locks. But their arguments were so compelling that I grew a beard one summer, and found that I liked it. When I got back to school at the end of August, I showed it off, then cut it before the first day of practice. "If I could cut my beard," I said. "You could do yours."

Lincoln Peddie, a Jamaican who grew up in England, also nudged me towards liberalness. He was a consummate professional who happened to shun hair clippers. Peddie was the kind of fellow who slipped a note under your door if he had an exam and thought he might be one minute late for practice. He was always the first to arrive at training and the last to leave. He was a wise 20-year-old who spoke to me about a man's essence being on the inside, not the outside. It helped me to deal with players as they were, and to show them the same respect they showed me.

But I still didn't like long hair on the playing field.

"We understood from Jump Street that Lincoln was a soldier man and we needed that discipline. Sometimes we buck 'im and 'im doh bow![30] And we respect 'im for that. Because at the end of the day, if you in trouble, who you going to talk to? Man used to talk to 'im about 'im girlfriend! 'Im was the godfather and 'im was the disciplinarian. I am so fortunate 'e was in my life. But 'im piss me off at times when 'im make some changes on the field."

---

[30] Didn't budge when opposed.

Keith "Barnaby" Tulloch, Jamaica (Howard Bisons, 1972-75)

"Lincoln had a very strict dress code. Some people couldn't abide by it. If we were taking a bus ride—eight hours to Clemson University in South Carolina—we had to come in a jacket and tie to go in that bus for eight hours. It wasn't so much about the jacket and tie; it was about recognizing his authority firstly, and secondly, representing black people properly. Every time we set foot off campus, we were representing black people."

Keith Look Loy, Trinidad (Howard Bisons, 1972-75)

"There is this thing called a team concept, where individualism and ego have to be set aside. The younger ones and the Jamaicans, we had to put them under heavy manners. The Africans—Sierra Leoneans, Guineans, Nigerians, Ethiopians—we had to blend them into being a team. Coming from foreign, they had to be acculturated."

Ernest Skinner, Trinidad (Howard Bisons team manager, 1967-72)

Some habits, I just had to deal with. Keith Aqui smoked. I'd turn a corner and he'd palm the cigarette, but a cloud of smoke haloed his head. "Man, you must be think I am a real jackass in truth," I mumbled as I walked away. Worse was when he ran past me on a game day at Mt. St Mary's in 1971 and I caught a whiff of alcohol. I told the drinkers on the sidelines   Keith's fans and friends—that if they liked him so much, they should have bought him a steak. Unfortunately, the guy went crazy that day. We won 13-3. Keith, who scored in nine out of ten regular season games that year, bagged eight. "In hindsight," I told him. "I would have let you come drunk for every game."

Then there was Ian Bain—vice-captain of the grousers. Ian had come to Howard from Trinidad via England. He liked to talk tactics, and there were many things he didn't agree with. His initial attitude was that soccer in America was no good. Because he was so fit, he tore up and down the pitch, refusing to hold his position in midfield. I pulled him aside at practice while the others scrimmaged. "You see these guys," I said, pointing. "They name 'defenders.' You see these guys: They name 'forwards.' Your job is to help the defenders, and give the forwards the ball when they make a run." I told him that if he wanted to run from end to end, he could play right wing—forging forward to cross balls when we were attacking, and dropping back to help when our defence was under pressure. He grumbled. What can I say? Habits. He played the position, and played it well, until he was returned to midfield.

For a long time, I had been an indifferent student. Not apathetic, just mediocre. Around age ten, I got lost in school. Our neighbour in St James, Clifford Lau—an apparently monogamous family man who'd once had his gerberas nicked by a couple well-meaning urchins—did his best to impart a little basic arithmetic to me from time to time, but never quite succeeded. By the end of a lesson, my head swimming with numbers, Lau would ask a simple question: "Five times five?" In utter frustration, I often blurted something silly: "Green!"

Fortunately, I liked to read. When my grandfather's eyes began to fail, he bribed me with a shilling to sit and read him the *Evening News*. The more I read to Dada, the easier it became and the more I enjoyed it. It should have been no surprise then when I graduated from QRC after two years with only a single O' Level pass, in English Literature. One secondary school pass out of eight! How on earth would I manage at the tertiary level?

The answer was with the help of my players. In my first few years at Howard especially, I coached a bunch of bright guys who were deadly serious about academics. They rode to games with their books and when the bus returned to campus at 10 and 11 o'clock at night, quite a few asked to be dropped at the library, where morning sometimes found them drooling on their books. Compared to most other athletes on campus, the soccer players were much in demand by campus administration for staffing campus events. Admin found them reliable and able to follow instructions. For years, they boasted a group grade point average over 3.0. Quite a few went on to become teachers, school principals, doctors, engineers, and lawyers.

In class, working towards a degree in physical education, I was getting 'C's. My players were getting 'A's. They did what they could to pull me through. One of my teaching aides was midfielder-turned-right-wing Ian Bain—forward Alvin Henderson's ball-supplier from St Mary's College. So intent was Alvin on having Ian join him at Howard that he had conducted secret negotiations with his friend, eventually convincing him that his education and footballing future lay on this side of the pond rather than in Europe. I took Alvin's word about Ian's skill and brought him to DC in 1971.

Ian was helping me translate a paragraph for my basic Spanish class one day and suggested a question to impress my teacher, the very *simpatica* Dr. Donahue. "*¿Que te parece a ti el clima?*" I said to Dr. Donahue when I had the chance. For the level I was at, this was quite an advanced way of asking what she thought of the weather. "*¡Oh, Felipe!*" she gushed, jotting a note in her little book. I got a B in the class.

In class, I had to humble myself, but in football I was the parent. In the National Soccer League, my players were leaning on me. For years, I refereed in the rough-and-tumble amateur division, supplementing my coaching and playing earnings with games on frozen pitches. (Soccer was not a mainstream sport; its season was scheduled for winter when the fields weren't in use for other sports.) Teams formed along ethnic lines, and in the early years when the Trinidad All Stars boasted a core of Trinidadians supplemented by Jamaicans and Guyanese, there was sure to be a fight if they came up against a team from Central America, the British Lions, or the Italian Cadets. The guys knew if I was the boss, they had some protection. Otherwise, they felt they were playing against twelve men, as some white referees made calls that bore no connection to reality or reason.

I tried to be fair. Before each match, I took out the red and yellow cards, flourished them for all to see, and stuck one in each sock. No warnings! But my refereeing days ended after a game between Italian Cadets and a Jamaican team. The Jamaicans boasted a couple brothers whose bodies seemed to have been forged from iron. I had recruited Richard "Real Kill" Davy for Howard on a tour to Jamaica; his brother Kenneth "Dirty Harry" Davy joined me later. Tall and slender, Dirty Harry theorized that his bones had been hardened by playing with bigger players, including his older brothers, and repeatedly being kicked into the goal with the ball.

A strange trend had taken hold in the league—the thumping of referees. After a foul, the players crowded the ref from all sides. He would never know who had punched him in the back of the head. In the match between the Italians and Jamaicans, I warned that I wasn't going to take a lash from anyone.

First, a guy toe-punched a ball into me very deliberately. Later, after I'd awarded a penalty, an Italian player rushed me with blood in his eyes. I swung my right so hard I'd have broken it if it connected. "Touch my COACH?!?" roared Real Kill, who had grabbed a corner flag as a mass of punching, kicking bodies converged. Dirty Harry ran wild, frothing, his jugular veins standing out on his neck. It was the last game I refereed in the league.

I had four sons of my own, but each year it seemed I acquired a few more. The West Indians and Africans were a long way from home, and I was an authority figure they trusted. They also loved me because I took them home for feeding. "What? Lincoln, I do not have food for twenty men!" protested Linda, when I called on short notice to say that the gang was coming. Somehow, she always found enough.

The Nigerians, in particular, were ever-hungry. Striker Kenneth Ilodigwe, who ate at the Howard cafeteria using coupons given to scholarship players, was fond of saying that he could eat twenty pancakes, and was never satisfied by insubstantial American food: "In Afreeca, we swallow big food." Linda never put the food on the table for the boys to help themselves. Some would have gorged themselves while others starved. But they were never shy about asking for seconds. "And this time," suggested one bold athlete, "Can you put a little more emphasis on the meat?"

I knew that some of the things I did outside the strict delineation of my coach's job were appreciated, but I did not find out how much a small act of kindness could mean to a player until many years later.

It was a cold, drizzly day in December 1971 and we were playing our bitter rivals Navy in the regional quarter-final. This was the year we went all the way to the first of two championships. My forward Mori Diane from the West African nation of Guinea was having a great game, and we won 3-0. After the match, I ran onto the field, took off my coat, and draped it over Mori's shoulders. There were ten other drenched men on the pitch, but for some reason, I went straight to Mori.

It was not until decades later that I learnt what the coat had meant to Mori. The day of the match, he had gone to the Guinean embassy in Washington DC, picked up a newspaper and read that his father, a government official, had been arrested in Guinea. For anyone anywhere, this would not be good news. But Mori knew immediately that his father could be tortured and killed. Guinea's president Sékou Touré had established a prison called Camp Boiro, where thousands of political opponents were being hanged or starved to death. Mori had come to America via Europe, where his father had sent him because he was concerned about the political situation in Guinea.

Mori later told me that he cried a lot that day because he felt so alone. He says that nothing could have been as comforting as that gesture. Placing the coat on his back had signaled that he would be alright. At the time, I only saw him as needing a little warmth.

7—THE MOST ODIOUS WORD

Howard University, Washington DC
1971

Let me shock you with a word: Nigger. I'll spare you the indignity from now on, but I can assure you that on an American soccer pitch in the 1970s, that string of vowels and consonants, arranged just-so and bearing the odious power of centuries of accumulated hate, was not uncommon. We heard it from the stands: "Damn, those n—s can run!" And we heard it on the field, where it was used as a cheap psychological ploy to throw us off our game. We heard it and we hated it. Sometimes it made us mad; sometimes it motivated.

I urged my players not to respond to race talk, but in the heat of the moment, some lost the struggle. You couldn't count on the refs to stop the epithets either. In those days, there were two referees rather than a ref and two linesmen. "We are playing against thirteen men," I'd say. "But if it's 5-0, the ref can't do anything about it." In the 1971 championship-winning season, powered by a goal-scoring competition between Keith Aqui and Alvin Henderson, we bagged 86 goals in 15 games. We conceded only nine.

At a game in West Virginia in 1973, Jamaican defender Bancroft Gordon was assigned to mark an ungentlemanly winger who jabbed and poked and tossed around the n-word. After crossing a ball, he smirked. "Got you that time, n—." The word was still forming on his lips when Bancroft hit him an elbow in the chops. Bancroft was sent off, and a 2-1 lead turned into a 3-2 loss. When we got on the bus, I looked him straight in the eye, ready to blast him for his intemperate act. "Don't worry," he rushed. "Lesson learned." He never even came close to getting a red card again.

But much of the racism was less obvious. Tireless Ian Bain, a man of fair complexion, was once taunted on the pitch: "Did your mother take a black man, or was it the other way around?" Other incidents resulted from farcical oversight. In 1968 before I took over as coach, the team went off to a tournament in Akron, Ohio. On the Saturday night before the final, the host school held a little get-together. When it dawned on them that the white girls wouldn't, or couldn't, dance with black men, the hosts rushed off to find black women. It was especially disconcerting to travel to West Virginia, where you were likely to glance up on the hill overlooking the field and see the silhouette of the archetypal redneck, clutching a moonshine jug with a shotgun hoisted over his shoulder.

When I arrived at Howard, most of the top local universities avoided us. They just didn't want to play a bunch of n——. It was not the thing to do. And due to NCAA rules, they didn't have to. The association ranked the teams, allowing the schools to set their own schedules. Only when we busted into the top four in our region were we guaranteed games against the top three, according to NCAA rules.

But even when we improved to a point where they could no longer ignore us, oh, they used every trick in the book to avoid it! The first complaint was that the school was in the ghetto. There ain't no denying, the 'hood was rough. Everything was for sale in the university's immediate vicinity—prostitutes, hot jewels, snatch-n-grab stereos—but I argued strongly that the character of the neighbourhood shouldn't deny us home-field advantage. Then they had a problem with the pitch. We played on a multi-purpose field shared with the football team, field athletes, and others. The grounds staff had a hard time keeping grass on it, and it was commonly known as the Dust Bowl. The Dust Bowl, I tell you!

In my early years, the University of Maryland did its best to stay away from having to play on a substandard pitch, in the ghetto, in front of black fans—despite the fact that the NCAA rankings obliged them to. They filed a complaint with the NCAA about the Dust Bowl and offered to meet on neutral territory. "We will play the game on our campus," I told their coach firmly. The day before NCAA inspectors arrived to survey our field, I got the groundsman to deal with a little problem: A long-jump pit with an asphalt run-up track that happened to be on the field. He leveled and graded for hours. When the NCAA inspectors arrived, they enquired about the pit. "You see any?" I asked, a look of innocent disbelief plastered across my face. The match was played at home.

In 1970, Naval Academy had us at their mercy on their home field for a playoff match in December. The day before the game, their coach told the *Washington Post*: "I hope the weather falls below 25 degrees so it can freeze the *you-know-whats* off those Jamaicans and Africans." It was so cold on the day of the match, my words stuck to my tongue. Navy very deliberately locked us out of their dressing rooms and we were forced to hustle to our bus for a little warmth at half-time. The boost we needed that day came in the form of the Howard marching band, which appeared from nowhere in the second half, stocked with long-legged girls. We froze our *you-know-whats* off, and won 2-0.

Navy avoided playing us at the Dust Bowl until they couldn't anymore. In 1971, they were greeted at the Howard campus by the menacing sound of African drums and a pumped-up crowd that knew all about the icy lockout. For some of the young West Indian and African players who had failed to grasp the racial significance of Howard's rise, this was the match that made it all sink in. At last, blacks were being met on equal terms. At last, we had the upper hand. For a change, the white team was less than 100% comfortable. I am not referring to anything more than home-field advantage, but what a splendid advantage it was.

"We have them here and we will grind them to dust," I said. "They will pay a dear price for what they did to us last year." My players knew, for the most part, that the way to retaliate was to put the ball in the back of the net while avoiding cheap fouls and red cards. The drums pounded across the Dust Bowl and we were quicker to every ball. My team was never inclined to elaborate play or excessive individual indulgence, but on that day, we were swept away by enthusiasm. We were playing for ourselves, for Howard University, and for black people in general. After we'd taken a comfortable 2-0 lead, I gave the signal the crowd wanted to see—thumbs up. Now, the boys could beat,[31] threading the ball through opponents' legs and enjoying a few tricks.

---

[31]   Deke, dribble.

After we'd thumped them, the Howard *Hilltop* reported: "It was revealed that Navy does not play Howard during the regular season for reasons which could not be disclosed by Navy's coach. Howard's Keith Aqui responded by saying: 'I guess it's because they don't like to lose.'"

We rampaged to the final four in 1971, as we had in 1970 where we'd lost in the semi-final. The press immediately kicked some sand in our faces, calling us "upstarts." If any team in the final four deserved to be labeled as if they'd appeared from nowhere, it was Harvard; they hadn't been to the finals before. But Harvard wasn't black and uppity.

I can't fully explain how racially sensitive we were at the time. On campus, people saw most things in racial terms, whether they were or they weren't. Calling us upstarts was just as good as calling us n—s. And if my boys didn't understand that we were playing for everyone of African ancestry, Dom Basil Matthews got the message through.

Dom Basil was a priest and football visionary. He'd been principal of a Catholic secondary school in Trinidad, where he recruited underprivileged boys to play the game and brought in coaches from Suriname and Brazil to polish their skills. His recruits formed the core of the national team for a generation. He was keenly aware of race. He had once noted that Queen's Royal College, the school that welcomed me as a boy who could play, was not originally meant for coloured people at all. It had been built, long before independence, for the offspring of the English and French creoles—the white island-born elite who clung to political and economic power thanks to the colonial system.

I always made a point of having insightful lecturers speak to the players. Dr. Dom Basil Matthews was now a professor at the School of Social Work at Howard, and I wanted him to inspire the team before the playoffs. Sitting in a classroom, they listened intently as the Dom held forth on the Triangle of Blackness, which he described as stretching from Africa to the Caribbean to North America. He said that little Howard University sat at the centre of that triangle, binding together the Pan-African struggle for civil rights.

We were at the epicentre of a global civil rights struggle! It was our job to instill pride. We were ambassadors of our race, he said, and ambassadors must be at their best—not often, but always. What is Pan-Africanism? On this field—African and Caribbean people, surrounded by their American brothers; the Triangle of Blackness, condensed into a university stadium. We emerged from that room fired up, our minds transformed by a dawning recognition of our small role in a global struggle. We knew now that by winning a championship, we would strike a blow against injustice.

At the championship banquet on the Friday night before the games, the team squared its shoulders and stood at full height. Twenty-four of us entered the banquet hall dressed in colourful African dashikis. (We couldn't find twenty-four robes in the same pattern, so we'd bought three sets of eight.) Heads turned as the team strutted through the hall to our seats. You could see the wheels turning: "Why the hell did we invite these people here in the first place?" I'd opposed the dashiki plan; I was a suit-and-tie man! My guys were revolutionaries. But after we'd debated it, I had approved.

I felt proud in my African garb.

In 1971, artificial turf was a relatively new invention. Playing on it was like running on carpet-covered concrete. And if you fell, you'd certainly leave some skin behind; the texture was like sandpaper. It also played differently to grass—the ball didn't slow down, and it bounced a bit more. The key while playing on artificial turf was to stay on your feet (to avoid being skinned) and to pass directly to foot (so the ball didn't scoot away from your target). To prepare for the Astroturf at Florida's Orange Bowl where the playoffs were held, we'd used the Washington Redskins' football field a couple times, and also the National Armory.

The day before we left for the finals in Florida, I proposed a grueling set of shuttle runs "for posterity." Back and forth the players sprinted, for the length of the entire Armory field. Now, if you've ever done a set of shuttles, even over twenty-five yards, you know that the exertion can leave you gasping like a fish out of water. This was the king of all shuttles. When we'd finished, the players collapsed. The Howard marching band, sitting in the stands waiting to rehearse, stood and applauded lustily.

We scraped through the semi-final against Harvard 1-0 on a goal by Ian Bain, but the game had been scrappy. The coach of our opponent in the final, St Louis University, claimed not to have been impressed by the quality of play. "Both of them looked so bad," said Harry Keough, "my number one problem may be getting my boys up for the finals." Keough had reason enough to dismiss the opposition. His team, the NCAA's defending champion, had played forty-four games unbeaten and was looking for its third consecutive championship. The players were so confident, they'd proposed wearing socks of different colours—one blue, one white. Keough convinced them it was not a good idea.

The city of St Louis, Missouri had a grassroots soccer program unrivaled in the United States. It was one of a few hotbeds in the country. Twenty-five thousand kids from kindergarten to high school played the sport, feeding the university with home-grown talent. What Keough didn't know might have made him even cockier: Keith Aqui, my galloping forward, had fallen ill after the semi-final. The doctor recorded a temperature of 102 and advised Aqui not to play in the final the next day. He was shivering and could barely move. (The origin of this illness is still a mystery. Aqui believes that he a chemical used on the turf got into his body when he fell and scraped his knee.)

For the final, we met a pitch marked for American football. The lines of a soccer field had been drawn over it. In the stands were our traveling supporters, many of them from the West Indies, along with a few members of the Howard faculty. On the sidelines, pretty Howard cheerleaders in short skirts bobbed and pranced. The starting eleven was seven Trinidadians, two Bermudans, one Guinean, and one Ghanaian. Keith Aqui was on the bench, sick. Our team was black; theirs was all white.

After five minutes, we had already conceded one. But it didn't take long to get it back. Striding into the box, Alvin Henderson tripped on the ball as he tried to get past the diving keeper. Fortunately, the goalie's momentum carried him past Alvin, who was now lying on the ground in the six-yard box with the ball at his feet. Flat on his butt, Alvin swung his leg and connected, knocking the ball past three St Louis defenders to score. St Louis then went ahead again with a bullet of a shot that keeper Sam Tetteh of Ghana only moved for after it had passed him.

I cannot express my relief at seeing my top goal scorer Keith Aqui warming up on the sideline. His fever had broken, and he insisted he was well enough to play. (He denies that he begged me to go on, his eyes misting over with tears.) I was certainly desperate enough to use him. One of our players had heard coach Keough say: "All they have is a long ball to Keith Aqui." Keough knew he was a threat and was bound to double-up on marking him, which would leave gaps in the St Louis defence.

The horn blew for the substitution, and the Howard band struck up a samba that the bandmaster had included especially for us. As Keith ran on, he looked ten feet tall. I felt as if the lights dimmed, and then brightened to a dazzling luminescence. He had two good chances that lifted the entire team. My Guinean forward Mori Diane, whose father had been carted away by a dictator's henchmen weeks before, evened it up for the second time with a close-range shot from a difficult angle. The score was 2-2.

It could have gone either way. St Louis had a slight advantage on the exchanges after that. And I soon found myself with a problem in defence, when experienced defender Rick Yallery-Arthur went down. Lying on the pitch with a dislocated shoulder, he could barely move. We carted him off and replaced him with another warrior. Thankfully, Alvin Henderson had another trick in him. Bermudan Stan Smith laid off a ball just outside the box, and Alvin dutifully whacked it home (one of those shots that seems not to deviate as it flies from boot to target) putting us ahead for the first time, 3-2. Somehow, we staved off St Louis's all-out attack that followed, and the final whistle blew.

What did I think as my players hoisted me atop their shoulders and I buried my face in my hands? You ask a difficult question. Perhaps I did not think so much as feel. I felt relief, and wonder, and joy. It was 1971, and we had become the first historically-black college to win an NCAA championship in any sport. We had fulfilled our role as custodians of the Triangle of Blackness.

The obvious move was to head straight back from Florida to Washington, DC. The city was starved for sporting success of any kind and they were dying to fete us. But we had a great invitation that I couldn't turn down: Howard's Jamaican alumni had invited us to visit Jamaica to play three games—one against a combination of the two best first division teams in the country. Twenty-two players voted to go to Jamaica. Two voted to go back to DC. Ian Bain grumbled that he had exams and had to study, but was heckled into submission by the enthusiastic majority. We dressed him, and everyone else, in green and black dashikis, and boarded a plane to Kingston.

Michael Manley, who went on to win an election and become prime minister not long after our Jamaica trip, came to congratulate us. He would have liked what he saw: Some of the best Caribbean minds, Afro-conscious and disdainful of suits. (Manley went on to scrap the requirement for jackets and ties in the Jamaican parliament. He preferred a Kariba suit himself, which was more comfortable in tropical weather.) We were big news! Our success reflected well not only on a hallowed African-American institution, but on the Caribbean and Africa as well.

Playing dreadfully, we narrowly beat the University of the West Indies in our first game. The studious Ian Bain, who I'd told not to dress, was sitting on the bench eating nuts when I told him to kit up, and sent him on to help avert impending disaster. The second match was against the combined first division teams, and there was a big crowd of Rastafarians in attendance.

When Alan "Skill" Cole, one of the best players Jamaica ever produced, was announced five minutes into the match and raised his hands above his dreadlocked head, the fans went crazy. They had also buzzed before the game, when the commentator introduced Howard goalkeeper Amdemichael Selassie from Eritrea (then part of Ethiopia). The rastas, of course, worship Ethiopian monarch Emperor Haile Selassie as the son of God. After the match, everyone wanted to meet our Selassie, and the rastas invited him to their commune. "You have to ask Coach about that," he said politely, and promptly disappeared. Selassie was no rasta, and wasn't quite ready for an evening of adulation.

Alan Cole, who went on to play for Brazilian club Nautica, took some warm kick[32] in the match, and we beat the combined team quite badly. He commented after the game: "This eh no bway (boy) ball. This big man game." After that, the level of play deteriorated, as I eased the reins so the boys could relax. They were in Jamaica, after all.

Our final game was against an All-Jamaica schoolboys team. This squad boasted a couple teenagers who brought my stalwart defenders to their knees. I was especially astounded by the little #10, who could

---

[32] Was the recipient of several robust tackles.

beat a man in a phone booth. "Who is that?" I asked after we'd lost 2-1. Richard "Real Kill" Davy was the response. Well, there was no way I was letting this little fish grow into a man-eater on some other team that we might one day have to face. The next day, I found myself searching for the parents of four Jamaican schoolboys. I asked the guardians of Bertram Beckett, Mario Mc Lennan, Keith "Barnaby" Tulloch, and Richard "Real Kill" Davy the same question: "Would your son like a scholarship to attend Howard University?" The answer in each case was a hearty yes. I was losing two players from my championship team, but I'd just restocked with four potential game-winners. The quality of our team had already improved.

On the plane out of Jamaica, the pilot announced: "We have traveling with us today, the NCAA winners, Howard University's soccer team." The passengers clapped. We landed at National Airport on the outskirts of Washington DC in a torrential downpour. The pilot came over the speakers again to say that we were supposed to go to Terminal A, but he'd taxi to Terminal B to let us out first. (Federal Aviation Administration regulations weren't quite as strict as they are today.)

Descending the mobile stairway, I saw Linda in the crowd of hundreds who had come to greet us. A Howard administrator held an umbrella over her as she rushed out to kiss me. Howard president Dr. James Cheek told the assembled that the team's victory was a victory for black people everywhere. A motorcade with police escorts led the honking entourage the few miles from National Airport to the Howard campus. In the Cramton Auditorium, five hundred fans led by the cheerleaders and the marching band, hooted and whistled as the team was presented. Mayor-commissioner Walter Washington said: "It's not too often we get a winner here in the District so that when we do, you have to be willing to share it a little."

We were honoured soon after with a banquet at the Sheraton Hotel. Among the handful of community organizations and university clubs to present us with awards were the Caribbean Student Association and The Pigskin Club of Washington, which was an American football association that believed in "good, clean sport." Programs were printed, and under the heading: **1971 National**

Collegiate Soccer Champions, the names of all the players were listed. Just below that, the program says: **Lincoln A. Phillips, *Coach.***

In the post-match euphoria, I had a little fun with the boys, picking up the locker-room phone and saying, deadpan: "Ah, Mr. President, I'm disappointed; I thought you would call sooner." The day after the win, however, I did get a telegram from President Richard Nixon. It offered us "heartiest congratulations" and said that we had made Washington very proud. The city had gone twenty-five years without a professional or collegiate champion. The Howard administration soon relayed an invitation to visit the White House, and I called a meeting to discuss the offer.

I was dying to go. I might never get a chance like that again. But some of the players weren't having it. They considered it an opportunity to stand up against injustice and let the administration know that black people would not be expediently used. From the perspective of a Howard student at the time, Nixon's civil rights record was atrocious. (The record shows that he desegregated Southern schools and implemented affirmative action.) The student body approved of our decision to decline the invitation. "You can't afford to let people ride your back," one student told me. "And the only way they'll ride you is if you bend."

After the championship, Howard offered me a full-time coaching position at a salary of $32,000 a year. Until then, I had been earning a stipend of a few thousand dollars. Playing pro soccer, I had earned $7,000 at most.

Our two sons were still in Trinidad living with their grandparents. Eating at a restaurant one night, Linda told me a story about her recent trip to Trinidad. She said she'd been having a conversation with a neighbour—within earshot of four—or five-year-old Sheldon. The neighbour asked how soon Linda would be returning to the United States. She turned around to see Sheldon crying. On hearing the story, I cried too. "That's it," I said. "As soon as we have the money for passage, bring my children up."

8—STRIPPED

Howard University, Washington DC 1972

For the players, being number one was a boon. The guys were very popular with the ladies. The sororities auctioned dates with hand-picked soccer players. Even our non-playing manager crowed about getting his fair share. Howard's campus was like any other tertiary education institution's—there was lots of sexual tension and, undoubtedly, lots of sex. And it wasn't only the Howard campus where our boys were stars. Whenever we traveled to a school with a small number of black students, they turned out to cheer for us rather than the home team. The women always cheered harder.

Such popularity could be a headache. No one wants to be the coach who chases potential conquests from the rooms of his testosterone-charged players. The task, however, occasionally fell to me. Staying at a hotel before a game, I found Bain and Henderson barefoot, raising a ball outside a room. "Where the other fellas?" I asked. They half-heartedly claimed not to know. Then the hotel room door opened. Out gushed music and high-pitched laughter. The African-American girls from the opposition university had come to check out the notorious Howard team. I was angry. I may have cried as I lectured them. "You don't get it," I said. "This thing is bigger than us."

But I did occasionally attend my players' parties, and I certainly knew quite a bit about their social lives. A nameless player once begged me to sneak him out of the bowels of the gym from my office. There were two women waiting for him in the lobby. Neither knew about the other. Another young woman once came to me and said that she liked "the one with the bushy hair"—goalkeeper Trevor Leiba. I said that for the right price, I could help her make a move. They were later married.

American students had also taken note of us and our sport. Rock Newman, a Howard baseball player who had grown up in rural Maryland, later acknowledged that he and his clique had considered us foreigners at first. We were "Others" who played a sport they didn't know and didn't understand. But our record of wins and losses made Rock take note. From his vantage point as an athlete, he knew the sweat and tears we were putting in at practice. The third baseman started trying to schedule his classes around soccer games, and became a "friggin fanatic." He said the soccer players looked like gazelles as they sprang onto the field, and he could scarcely believe how fast we were to the ball in comparison to our opponents. "Once their excellence was executed and demonstrated on the field," says Rock, "they became brothers."

Howard had taken the decision in 1970 to use sports to attract students and funding. In my two years at the university, I had gained good ground for the team and myself. I was employed full-time, soccer players no longer wore baseball socks, and they all ate for free thanks to university meal vouchers. Administrators had come to rely on the soccer players to work at on-campus events. They were reliable. But soccer still didn't rank very high on the sporting food chain. It rankled to see bumper stickers on campus that said: "Let's make football and basketball #1!" We were already #1, but we weren't getting as many scholarships as the "premier" sports. Thankfully, I always had friends in high places.

Katherine Green worked in the Financial Aid Department. "Linc, this is not fair," she said. "You all should be getting more scholarships." Who was I to disagree? We'd won the championship and we still didn't get equal support. Katherine went to her boss Goldie Claiborne and came back with a deal that made up for the shortfall in athletic scholarships: "As long as your players maintain a three-point average (a 'B'), they'll get a tuition waiver." I had a studious bunch of players at the time. Several qualified easily for tuition waivers, freeing up the athletic schols so I could recruit to strengthen the team that everyone would be gunning for.

I had a couple friends on the teaching staff as well. Wolsey Semple lectured in the Engineering department. Semple, from Guyana, was a lifelong fan of the game. He remembered seeing me in Guyana as a 19-year-old goalkeeper playing for a pick-up team from Trinidad. I'd been reading a newspaper during the game. (We were dominating the Guyana national team and I leaned against the goalpost to read a comic strip. I liked to make a little style for the fans.) Semple came to almost every game we played, and he strongly suggested that his students attend too. One of his students, a former player who could no longer make the cut, badly wanted to see us play in the 1971 final in Florida but couldn't find the money. Semple found him a job in the computer lab that earned him just enough to make the trip.

And then there was trainer Milton Miles. If you have a soldier you want to punish, you send him to the outpost. He could have considered it exile to be assigned to the soccer team rather than football or basketball. Milton, however, embraced us. He took his time taping sore ankles and knees so the padding was smooth, and ferreted out little caches of sports drinks instead of always giving us water. After one of my professional games against Pelé, where I spent ninety minutes under fire from every angle, I returned to campus bruised and aching. I approached Milton, intending to ask him to fire up the hot tub. "Milt . . ." I said. "It's ready," he interrupted. He'd been expecting me.

As much as the players enjoyed uplifting me in class, they relished any opportunity to humble me on the field. I gave them the chance when I was simultaneously coaching Bowie State College—that terrible bunch led by the fat goalie, Chick—and Howard. Bowie, who played in a nothing-league, had begged for the privilege. When the NCAA champion Howard players laughed at the suggestion, I threw out some bait: "I am going to be in goal." They gobbled that up.

The day of the match, I bawled at my defenders to mark the two All-American Howard forwards, Alvin Henderson and Keith Aqui. Poor defenders, they were playing a whole different class of opposition. Like hail, the ball came at me from every angle. Those wicked fellas; I had never seen them shoot like that. I thought they were intent on hurting me. I must have played out of my skin but we conceded 13. It could have been 35.

In my last year of professional soccer, with the Baltimore Comets, I was approached by former player Mori Diane, who had recently turned pro with the Washington Diplomats. "Coach," he said (they all called me Coach, long after they had gone on to become doctors, lawyers, and teachers), "we go eat you up." The end of the season was fast approaching and the game meant nothing. I was coming to the end of my career. Mori was being a pest, taunting me relentlessly. Before the match, I approached the Comets coach. "Coach, I feeling a little twinge in the hamstring." He put my back-up Alan Mayer in net. Mori scored two and had one assist. (They still count assists in soccer in North American soccer today.) As expected, he came to my office to gloat. I was ready. "If I was in goal, those goals woulda never score," I said. "And if they didn't score, I would have been the cause of your disappointment, after coaching you for all these years." It was the only comeback I had that day.

In October 1972, halfway through the season with a team fortified by Jamaican additions, our 1971 championship success began to unravel. An NCAA investigator showed up on campus to speak to Keith Aqui. First, he wanted to know if Keith had played professionally for the Darts or Bays. The answer was no. "What's your GPA?" asked the investigator. It was 3.4, way above the minimum qualifying standard to play sports. The man then went into his folder and produced a record of every team my 25-year-old loping athlete had ever played ball for in Trinidad: St George's College, Notre Dame, Mausica Teachers' Training College, Shell. "Is there any professional soccer in Trinidad?" asked the investigator. "No," replied Aqui. "You buy your boots. You pay for your jersey. You not getting paid for anything." The stone-faced investigator nodded, picked up his files, thanked Keith, and left.

We understood then that a serious investigation was underway.

A disgruntled coach had written to the NCAA Infractions Committee, attaching a profile of Keith from the *Washington Post* and suggesting an inquiry into the eligibility of players in the Howard soccer program. His age, I assume, and the fact that he had played a lot of soccer, had been enough to prompt the NCAA to dig. The rule they hung Keith with said that a foreign student athlete forfeits a year of eligibility for each year of organized sport played in his own country after he turns 19. They said Keith's eligibility had expired in 1970, the year before the championship.

It was a crippling blow. Not only was I made to pull Keith off the team, but my nemesis, athletic director Leo Miles, wanted others benched too. The NCAA hadn't mentioned them. The association had a welter of rules concerning eligibility and was relentless in enforcing them. We all thought we knew who had sent the fateful letter to the NCAA. "I think the coach of Navy is just trying to get us out of the competition," I told *Ebony* magazine. "Soccer has always been a game dominated by white Europeans, and the local schools are a little jealous." The Navy coach, he of the infamous "freeze the *you-know-whats* off" media quip, was the obvious suspect. To us, it seemed that *white* foreigners were alright—the University of Maryland had won the championship with a team full of them—but *black* foreigners weren't. There were moves afoot, fueled by local coaches, to limit the number of foreigners playing on any college team.

In 1972, we got to the national semi-final once again and met the team we'd beaten the year before, St Louis. But five of our starters including Keith Aqui and Mori Diane had been declared ineligible or ordered not to suit up. We lost. I expected depression, but as we got off the bus, a calypso was jamming on an eight-track tape player and the boys began beating their boots. People would have thought we won!

On the Friday night at the awards banquet, however, I had the chance to speak my mind. First I thanked everyone and congratulated our opponents. "Today, I just want to tell you that St Louis did not beat Howard," I continued. "They beat the remnants of Howard." I accused the NCAA of racism. "Anytime a group of people get together to deprive another group of their rights," I said. "That is racism." All four teams stood to applaud. As I walked away from the podium, I met Keith Look Loy, one of our forcibly benched players. He was an articulate revolutionary, far to the left of the political spectrum. I apologized to him for my lack of eloquence. "Coach," he said, "to hell with the grammar. We are so damn proud of you."

Not long after my speech, the NCAA announced that it was stripping Howard University of our 1971 title. We were also being placed on probation for 1973, which meant we could compete in the regular season, but not in the playoffs. University president Dr. James Cheek said that the school intended to challenge the decision in court. He summed up everyone's feelings when he said: "We feel that it is simply because we are a black institution that the NCAA was requested to investigate the eligibility of our outstanding players."

"All of a sudden there's this black team challenging for supremacy, and that was not taken lightly by the people who were the traditional powers."
Rick Yallery-Arthur, 1971 championship team

"In a word, I thought it would have been overlooked if it was not an all-black institution. They were still the best team in the country."
Fred Schmalz, coach of Howard opponent, Davis & Elkins College

"We knew they would come after us. There was always a hint around that people felt we were cheating and that a number of us had played pro."
Alvin Henderson, All-American forward on 1971 team

"There was an exclusionary mindset, and it was just like: 'This wasn't supposed to happen, we're not accepting it, and we're going to find a way to take away the title you won on the field with a great victory.' These (NCAA) rules are so crazily written and so obscure that you could find something to take anybody's title away. I never accepted it. I was like, 'That's bull—.' You win the fight in the ring, you're the winner."
Rock Newman, Howard baseball player

"The intent was to clip the wings of the Howard soccer team; in particular to get Keith Aqui out of the lineup."
Wolsey Semple, Professor—Howard computer science department

One thing we knew was that our biggest rival, St Louis University, had not led the charge to have us investigated. After Keith Aqui had graduated and was playing professional soccer for the Baltimore Comets, he was called over by the coach of the opposing team, who introduced him to St Louis coach Harry Keough. Keough insisted that he hadn't seen the letter that started the NCAA investigation. He said, in fact, that he hadn't accepted the 1971 trophy, which had been taken from the office of the Howard University president and handed back to the NCAA so St Louis could be declared champions of 1971. It was good to hear that a man I admired and considered a worthy and honourable opponent had not approved of the way the NCAA had done things. At the time, however, the stripping hurt to the core.

I sometimes wonder if I was negligent in checking player eligibility. Today there is an NCAA Eligibility Center that reviews each and every prospective player's academic record and amateur status, but at the time there was no one to do it but me. I had to interpret all the NCAA rules, some of which seemed to have been variably enforced. I can tell you that I certainly never set out to cheat. Negligent is a hard word, but at the end of the day the buck stopped with me.

The one comfort I had was hearing every player from that history-making 1971 team repeat a version of the same thing: "Coach, they could take away the trophy as much as they want. We know that we are the real champions." I could imagine Coach Chambers, with his Howard University cap pulled snugly down on his bald head, saying in response to all that had happened: "Lord, help us to win. But if we lose, help us not to cry over spilt milk." If we did lose, he reminded us not to lose the lesson. It felt like we had won and lost simultaneously.

9—REVENGE

Howard University, Washington DC 1973

Oh, 1973! The hardest season I ever coached. For one, there was no playoff potential; the NCAA had put us on probation. It was hard keeping the guys focused. What were you playing for? There was nothing to win and nowhere to go.

My Guinean midfielder Mori Diane, still under NCAA suspension for failing to take the American SAT exam, wanted to play soccer so badly that he dropped out of Howard to turn pro. Tony Martin, the captain in 1972, decided he'd sit out the year and return in 1974. And All-American Alvin Henderson graduated in three years and went on to medical school. A regional rivalry—Jamaican versus Trinidadian—also added to my woes. There were whispers: "You better than Bain; 'ow 'e playing ahead of you? Is because 'e's a Trini." On the field, players preferred to pass to their countrymen.

Cultural differences exacerbated tensions. The Jamaicans didn't always appreciate the Trinis' sense of humour. On their way to practice one day, Ian Bain and Alvin Henderson stopped at a red light with a carful of Jamaicans behind them. The Trinis didn't move when the light turned green, and only pulled off as it was about to turn red again, stranding the Jamaicans for another turn of the light. The Jamaicans were vex for days. They also didn't appreciate picong.[33]

My one bright spot in a lost year was the acquisition of Jamaican Mikey Davey. I'd picked up Mikey's brother, Richard Real Kill, on the tour of Jamaica. Mikey had migrated to New York to live with his

---

[33] A stream of teasing banter.

sister, taken his SATs and scored high enough to get into most private universities. But he wanted to play soccer at Howard. He nagged his brother incessantly: "Real, did you check Coach Phillips about a scholarship for me?" Richard eventually told him to come down to Howard for the start of the 1973 season. For forty minutes during scrimmage, Mikey, a crunching tackler, held off my forwards. A guy tried to run past him, and he easily reeled him in. Negotiations for his scholarship were completed on the sideline.

When I said *one bright spot,* I truly meant it. At the University of Maryland, an opposition player spat on Jamaican Mario Mc Lennan. My rule was: Don't let the n-word throw you off, but if someone spits at you and you get a red card, don't expect me to be angry. Mario let the player have it, and fans from both sides rumbled onto the field. Someone prepared to attack the referee, who happened to be a friend of mine. "Don't touch him!" I shouted. He recounted my intervention to the media.

The long, messy, uninspired season came to a head in the mountains of West Virginia after a match against a lesser opponent. We had lost 1-0 to Davis & Elkins College. It was an ugly goal, mistakenly cleared into our own net by one of our defenders. On the bus, the Jamaicans laid into the hapless player. And then the bus broke down. Here we were, in the middle of the Appalachian Mountains, arguing about a lost season. No one was coming to get us anytime soon and we were on the verge of blows. When the angst had burnt off, the players sat outside the bus and talked. They concluded that they wanted to put everything right in '74. It was the next time we'd have a shot at the playoffs.

I'd been doing some research. One of my players, Nigerian Charlie Pyne, had suggested that I look to his homeland for talent. He referred me to the chairman of the Nigerian Football Association, Baba Shola Rhodes, who was happy to serve as my scout. Speaking long-distance over the course of a month, we winnowed a list of thirty players to six. "You see this player," Rhodes would say, "he is the best player in all of Nigeria. But you don't want him." He knew the players' attitudes, skills and temperaments, and would not have saddled me with a problem.

It was time to see the Nigerians firsthand, and I had to do it before the 1974 season began. I went to athletic director Leo Miles for the money to cover the trip. "$5,000?" he said. "NO!" (I'd once heard Miles wish against the volleyball team making the playoffs because he claimed not to have the money to fund their travel.) I hoped the vice-president of student affairs, Dr. Carl Anderson, would be more receptive. "Doc," I said, "If we get these six players, we win the championship." Everyone in campus administration, with the possible exception of Leo Miles, wanted revenge for the NCAA stripping of 1971. "Win the championship!" parroted Anderson. "Come for the cheque tomorrow."

In Nigeria, Shola Rhodes took me to club games and introduced me to players. I only found out later that the very athletes I was trying to recruit did their best to stay clear of him. It was rumoured that he was gay, and they were all quite homophobic. Being in Rhodes's company, they believed at first that I was also homosexual.

I'd sent the Nigerians detailed questionnaires on their favourite food, music, and movies. I also knew their nicknames in advance. "How you doing, Bonga?" I'd ask on meeting a player. "HUHHHHHH!!!" came the high-pitched response typical of some Nigerians. "How you know that?" My response was: "I know everything about you guys."

I was looking at top-class talent, and I was lucky that the professional European leagues were still essentially closed to Africans. For many Nigerian stars, playing at an American university was the best they could do.

All six who I targeted agreed to come to Howard on scholarship.

In defence, I got centre-back Dominic Ezeani, who played for Enugu Rangers and Nigeria; the midfield was strengthened with Sunny Izevbigie and Miyiwa Sanya; I found a good dribbler in Balotunde Balogun; and the forward line, depleted by the loss of my deadly striking duo Keith Aqui and Alvin Henderson, was boosted by Yomi "Bonga" Bamiro and Kenneth "Kendo" Ilodigwe. Apparently the question about my sexuality didn't bother any of them enough to keep them away.

Sunny Izevbigie, who played for the champion club, Vipers of Benin, says that as far as he knows, I was the first ever American coach to recruit in Nigeria.

Kendo arrived at the Howard campus with all his possessions in a box, which he carried on his head. The first person he met was trainer Milton Miles. "Put that box down," ordered Milton. "Don't carry a box on your head in America." Kendo had only ever played in oversized or undersized tugs.[34] At my home in Maryland, his "Momma," my wife Linda, cooked a meal for him, and Kendo asked for a pair of boots. I asked what kind he wanted, and he responded very precisely: "A World Cup '74." The man worshipped those boots. He said from the time he put them on, he knew he was "in a different kind of arena." I was reminded of myself, caring lovingly for the pair of Adidas cleats my sister had bought me as a young man.

At practice, another very solid player fell into my lap. A short guy, a little taller than the grass, came to my office and informed me that he was a full-back, the last line of defence on a soccer field. (Most full-backs are tall because they have to get up for aerial balls.) "You?" I said. "So short!" Not only was he a full-back, but he claimed to have played for the Ghanaian national team. This was too good to be true. I did my research at the Embassy of the Republic of Ghana, and put him through his paces on the pitch. All of it was true! His name was Samuel Tetteh.

The addition of six talented Nigerians and one Ghanaian proved one thing: Any previous tension between Trinidadians and Jamaicans had been a joke. We now had a real rivalry. The Nigerians had a harsh way of talking, and the Jamaicans were sensitive to perceived slights. Guys fought in the dressing room, and did well to keep it from me. But they couldn't always hide the evidence. Trinidadian Ian Bain stepped in to part a locker room fight once and took a serious right hand that left him with a black eye. As a captain, Bain, respected by his teammates, was instrumental in keeping a relative peace.

At practice, players who had represented their countries clashed for a spot on a college team. Nigerian Frank Oshin, of whom the Jamaicans said: "'im born from cast-iron" came up against an equally rugged Jamaican in practice one night. Like competing rams, they charged each other. From the sideline, the contact rattled my bones. At times, I cut practice short because it got too rough.

In 1971, I knew clearly who my starting eleven was going to be. Three years later there were sixteen or seventeen who could legitimately

---

34   Soccer shoes.

claim spots. And national players came with nation-sized egos. It wasn't unusual for me to end up with four players on the bench, each of whom had represented his country. I often took the biggest egos aside, telling them that they knew the team couldn't succeed without them. "I just need you to help out so-and-so," I'd say. "If you can give him the ball at the right time, we win."

I still remembered a couple tricks about asserting authority early, reinforced in my first year at Howard when knife-toting Billy Jones from Sierra Leone put down a dressing room cussing that would have burnt the hair out of your ears. I had waited for Billy to finish, and said quietly: "You are a university student and you are expected to express yourself in a proper manner. This is the last time you are going to use that language, or you are not going to play." The message for the team was: "When I am finished with you, you are going to need the nearest West Indian or African to hold onto, because I am going to bust your balls."

During preseason training, I ran them through the gently rolling hills around Howard until they vomited from exertion. No one is quite as feisty when he's doubled over, retching. When they did flutter kicks[35] to strengthen their abdominals, I would tell them, "For rest, just leave your legs up there." I'll admit I was a terror.

To win. That, above everything, motivated the 1974 team. And in tough moments, the cliquishness and national chauvinism evaporated. It was one love, and one unit. Dare not touch a part of that unit because they would turn on you like a snake!

On road trips, I shuffled the rooming assignments so players couldn't stick to their countrymen: Bain with Balogun, Davey with Bonga, Leiba with Sanya. Along the way, they discovered what they had in common. There were cultural similarities: Africans and West Indians both have rhythm and love to dance; they also enjoy some of the same food, albeit prepared in different ways. But at times, the West Indians were skeptical of African mystical practices.

In 1971, Nigerian Olosegun Onadeku told Ian Bain before the semi-final that Ian would score an important goal. He duly bagged the winner, burnishing the Nigerian's reputation as a soothsayer. Onadeku, who claimed to be a prince and had several wives simultaneously, also

---

35 Lying on your back, kicking your legs.

often asked players for their boots, which he anointed with strange balms. Before the final against St Louis, he placed little heaps of corn kernels on the locker room floor, prayed over them, and told his teammates to step on each pile on their way out. (This would require some awkward stretching.) Everyone looked at me for guidance. "You didn't hear what the man say!" I asked. "We eh leaving nothing to chance." We won the match.

Spoilt for skill in 1974, I had to cut both scholarships and players. On hearing that some of their schols would be reduced by as much as 25% when the Nigerians arrived, the Jamaicans came in a delegation led by *General* "Barnaby" Tulloch. I called him General because he commanded the field with a military presence. He had acquired the name Barnaby because he resembled a character from the musical *Mary Poppins*. This was no musical moment—the Jamaicans were angry! They argued that they'd been putting out their all, and deserved reciprocity.

"Listen," I said, "your argument is fair. But we have six players coming from Nigeria. If we get those six, we win the NCAA championship." I left the decision to them: Import only two Nigerians, allowing them to keep their full scholarships; or bring all six, which meant a cut. I reminded Mario Mc Lennan that I'd taken him off the field sobbing when we'd lost the 1972 semi-final against St Louis with a depleted team. It was lucky for me the Jamaicans wanted to win so badly.

But each time recruitment improved the quality of the team, I had to shuffle players around. Bermudan Stan Smith, in jeopardy of losing his spot after the introduction of the Jamaicans in 1972, had been moved three times—from the forward line, to midfield, to centre-back. And when I couldn't move a player to a different position or find space for him on the bench, I faced the unpleasant business of making cuts.

Charlie Pyne was the short, heavily muscled Nigerian walk-on who had referred me to Nigeria for players. He liked little touches and would try to flick a ball over a man's head just for style. In previous years, when we were leading and I wanted to give the fans a show, I'd put Charlie on the field. He was sure to hop all around the ball like a cicizeb,[36] putting on a show. Everyone loved him. The team had attended one of the 1971 championship banquets in traditional western wear—jackets and ties. Sure enough, Charlie had walked in

---

[36]   A little tropical bird, the male of which jumps repeatedly to attract a mate.

long after the appointed hour wearing dark shades, a headpiece, and a gown fit for an African king. In his hand, he held a broad fan.

There was no place for Charlie on the 1974 team. We were focused on pace and our ability to outrun and outdribble opponents. In the first two practice games, he didn't see the field. Neither did the "cast-iron" Frank Oshin, our leading goalscorer the previous year. Knowing what was coming, Charlie lay in wait for me at a team meeting held in the gym. He had a ball in his hand. "What the #&@% is going on here!" he began. "You drop me! Me? Charlie Pyne!" He booted the ball into the air, raised it a couple times, caught it on his instep, and flicked it softly away.

Charlie's salty language forced my hand. I needed no further excuse to cut him, and took the opportunity to get rid of a few others as well. The 1974 team was going to be the best college team ever to play on American soil. And we had a great motivator: Revenge.

10—LEATHER BULLETS

Baltimore, Maryland
1972

Basketball announcer Jim Karvellas thought he could bring professional soccer back to Baltimore. The Baltimore Bays had lost $1 million in three years of operation in the late '60s before folding (and sending me scrambling to play for the Washington Darts), but Karvellas—the voice of the NBA's Baltimore Bullets—planned to make pro soccer profitable by attracting more fans and refusing to pay "super salaries." He wanted me to play in goal, and play a major role in building the team.

Victor Gamaldo, my fellow T&T national team player, was also picked for the new-look Bays of 1972. Victor worked at a bank and had incipient knee problems, but was still pro-quality. As long as he wasn't lighting his eyebrows on fire while trying to cook for a bunch of immigrant soccer players, he was a good man to have around.

Apart from the three Trinidadians (ex-Howard player Rick Yallery-Arthur was also on the team), the Bays roster included a Ghanaian, a couple Jamaicans, some Englishmen and a couple Americans. Soccer was desperate for validation in the United States and there still wasn't very much high-calibre homegrown talent around. Hank Kazmierski, a 22-year-old forward who had made it onto the U.S. national team as an alternate, was one of the few natives to play for the Bays. He was often booed when he came on as a substitute. He ran a lot and threw away lots of chances, but could be very dangerous. The Englishmen, who came with superior attitudes, thought he was the worst thing ever. What I liked about Hank was that he knew how to get into scoring position; even if he wasted his chances more often than not.

The best thing Karvellas did with his new team was opt out of the struggling North American Soccer League. He decided—and it sounded like a gimmick to many at first—that we would play ten exhibition matches against foreign first division clubs. I was about to face a barrage of leather from the very best from Mexico, Germany, Russia, Great Britain, and Brazil. I would ultimately enjoy the task of trying to keep the mighty Pelé out of my net.

First came the Germans. Werder Bremen had just placed eleventh out of eighteen in the very competitive German First Division. On the left wing was Willie Neuberger who had represented Germany at the 1970 World Cup. We gave the 5,197 fans in attendance their fill. From the opening whistle, the ball went end to end. BAM! It hit the crossbar of the Werder Bremen goal. Four seconds later, it was whistling towards me like a rocket-propelled grenade. In the second half, I was on my back much too often. And at the opposite end, goalkeeper Dieter Burdenski was sweating profusely as he punched and dove. But the save that kept them talking after the 1-1 match was one of mine.

A Werder Bremen winger who I'd expected to cross the ball, instead took a shot at the near post. Because I was already committed to covering the middle of the goal, I only had one hand with which to deal with the ball, and somehow got enough on it to flick it behind my back, beyond the far post. "What the hell you just do there, Tiger?" said Victor Gamaldo, running back in defence. I shrugged.

It was an unorthodox save, dragged I suppose, from the depth of my memory where the circuitry for playing basketball was lodged. It must have resembled a behind-the-back pass. Yet, my fans had always insisted that I had the superhuman ability to change direction in mid-air.

"He did something that some of us who were there found impossible. He took a dive to the left and did a 360. It was one of those things where he didn't know what he did. Of course, some people might say it was obeah."

Fellow soldier Carl Alfonso on a North-South game at the Queen's Park Oval, Trinidad

"He used to change direction in the air! He used to give me heartache."

Malvern fan Trevor Mitchell, on watching me play for Maple in Trinidad.

"It deflected to the left and he was going one way, and changed direction and got his fingertips to it. It still scored. He was already going in one direction and swung back in the other direction."

Maple captain Sedley Joseph on an attempted save against Dynamo.

"He's easily the best goalie the Bays have had and I think he's the best of anyone who ever played in the league. Back when we were a member (of the North American Soccer League), Oakland had a good goalie (Mirko Stojanovic), but he had a real strong team behind him. He's never seen the moves Lincoln has."

Joe Speca, coach of the Baltimore Bays in 1972.

"He was almost catlike. On more than one occasion when I was playing against him, I would applaud some of his saves from the other end of the pitch. It would have been nice to have seen if he'd gone to play in England. I think he was maybe a bit ahead of his time. I think Lincoln, given the opportunity could well have played in Europe."

Goalkeeper Dick Howard, who played against me for the Rochester Lancers in the North American Soccer League in the early 1970s.

"He was a lot more agile than me, a lot more skill in terms of good springing and good diving, a lot more acrobatic. He was a good person to sit behind and watch do it for a while and say, 'OK, this is the way it should be played.'"

Goalkeeper Alan Mayer, who backed me up for the Baltimore Comets in 1974.

My basketball days had served me well in my professional career. I had learned to bound and "float" (it's called hang-time today) from Taffy Crichlow, one of Trinidad and Tobago's first floaters. The trick—and being fully aware of the laws of physics, I can only say that it's a trick—is to create the illusion of momentarily defying gravity by fully extending your body at the top of your arc.

Like every athlete, I had some great games in my career. I also played some stinkers. One of my best matches in a losing effort came for the Trinidad and Tobago team in Costa Rica. The game was played at high altitude and we hadn't had time to acclimatize. Soon all our players were winded, and the Costa Ricans swarmed our goal. We lost 4-0, but they should have scored fifteen. The day after the game, the team went into town. Some youngsters sitting on a curb gestured at us. "Team," they said, holding their noses and fanning away an imaginary stench. Then they gave us the thumbs-up. "Goalkeeper," they said, smiling.

Then there was the 5-2 mauling of the Bays by the German club Stuttgart. The word had apparently gone out that I was good, and the second German team on the schedule decided to test me from the very first. (They may also have been pissed that an upstart American team had drawn with Werder Bremen.) The first shot of the game was a thunderbolt from a long way out. It rattled the upright and rebounded into play. It also rattled me. Later in the match, my addled brain still dealing with the opening shot, forward Herbert Hoebusch booted a lazy ball into my arms. Somehow, it trickled through and rolled over the goal line. I heard Victor Gamaldo say, "Come on, guys. Linc having a bad day." I later told the press: "That never, never happened to me before. I lost sight of it for an instant. By then I couldn't recover."

Those Germans kicked the hell out of that ball. Bullets once again. The left winger beat my normally solid Jamaican fullback Winston Earle like a drum. First he came down the wing and crossed far post. Next, he rifled one at the near post that I had to come flying to save. Every time he attacked, he did something different. Then he decided he'd had enough fun on that side and switched to the right. Victor said quite rightly that "it wasn't one of my better games." I've never seen anyone kick the ball like that team.

Meanwhile, Baltimore boy Joey Speca, who had also played briefly for the Bays, was not quite living up to his title as coach. His pre-game talks often went like this: "Guys, this is a big game for us. We have to beat this team. Their record is such-and-such . . . Linc . . ." Of course, he expected me to take over from there. I had been coaching Regiment, the Darts, and Howard for so long that it was second nature to pick up where he left off.

As a boy, Soviet goalkeeper Lev Yashin had been my hero. He was huge, with giant fists that smacked the ball with a resounding POW! Now, I was due to meet Yashin in person, as coach of fearsome Soviet club, Moscow Dynamo. The Cold War was very much on, and the game held overtones of the capitalist/communist rivalry. Victor ran forward from central defence twice, and our winger slotted the ball back for him on both occasions. Both times, he threaded the ball past the Dynamo keeper. His second goal salvaged a 3-3 draw with 1:10 remaining in the match. According to one newspaper, ten thousand fans "practically shook the rafters off the stadium." In the locker room after the match, we clustered around Yashin for his autograph. I still have a picture of the two of us.

Really, in 1973 I wanted no more of Pelé. He'd scored four goals against me in 1970 when I was player-coach with the Washington Darts. The Darts were a very good team (good enough to make it in today's Major League Soccer, I dare say) and we wanted to be at our best to keep pace with Pelé's powerful Brazilian club Santos in a friendly match. The maestro was fresh out of the 1970 World Cup where he'd scored four and hoisted the Jules Rimet trophy aloft as the Brazilian squad, rated among the best ever, trounced Italy in the World Cup final 4-1. Early in the second half, the Darts led 4-3, and I had limited Pelé to one. Your boy was feeling good. Then the floodgates opened. In the space of twelve minutes, Pelé scored two with his head and one with his left foot. The man could jump higher, stay up in the air longer, and he thought quicker. Plus, his supporting cast was exceptional. I was proud to have shared a field with him.

Three years later, in 1973, Edson Arantes do Nascimento, known by all and sundry as Pelé, was back. The Bays had signed both my Howard University forwards, Keith Aqui and Alvin Henderson, and we continued to play foreign clubs. With Alvin sitting on the bench (the Bays had just beaten English club Bristol without him, and new coach Dennis Viollet said he didn't want to change a winning formula) Santos went up 5-0. Pelé had scored three in nine minutes. The press reported that I couldn't have stopped the third, drilled into the net from fifteen feet out, with a ten-foot pole. I did, however, get the better of the great man once. Not for the first time, he broke through my defence and had me one-on-one. I faked him in one direction, then went the other way, diving to snatch the ball from his feet. As I went down, I heard him shout in frustration. The next time he got through, I faked the hell out of him again. He took it. But at top-speed, he cut the ball back and slotted it past me. Obviously, that fake didn't work more than once on a man of such class.

Coach Dennis Viollet finally put Alvin on in the 61st minute. The boy scored three, and the crowd of 24,680 erupted. We lost 6-4, but in the euphoria of the goal-scoring blitz, the fans stripped Pelé of his shirt and shorts. Clad only in his black bikini underwear, he was hustled from the field by security. Viollet told the media: "He scored three times against us, so what? They've been trying to stop Pelé for fifteen years now and still no one has done it." Alvin Henderson, who had also scored three, sat by himself, mumbling about what a dream the day had been.

We played Santos twice more on their ten-game North American tour, which they finished unbeaten. In the final match, they earned a corner, which Pelé set up to take. They'd been taking them short, so I shouted for Jamaican defender Winston Earle to get out and cover it. Seeing that I was expecting a centering pass, Pelé curled one into the goal. I could possibly have saved it, but I would certainly have had a rude encounter with the post. "This is the first time I ever scored on a corner kick," said Pelé as he rushed off to catch a train to New York. I was honoured to have played against him, but no part of me regretted his departure.

I didn't earn very much playing for the Baltimore Bays, but the city was a great sports town, and the soccer team enjoyed the same notoriety as the NFL's Baltimore Colts, professional baseball's Baltimore Orioles, and the NBA's Baltimore Bullets. Many years after I'd retired from pro soccer, I was driving to my home in Maryland from Washington DC, when a cop pulled me over for driving with missing lights. He took my driver's license and studied it. "Lincoln Phillips?" he said. "Goalkeeper with the Bays?" Yes, I answered, thinking that this might end better than I'd feared. With his foot on my bumper, he reminisced about our matches against Pelé. Finally, he wrapped up. "It's dangerous to drive like that," he said. "I'll drive in front of you."

11—TRUTH

Howard University, Washington DC 1974

We needed a slogan for our 1974 season. For stripping our 1971 title, for forcing us to bench some of our best players in 1972, for making us play a meaningless 1973 season, we wanted *revenge*. Yet it was too crude a word to inspire. I needed something else.

In the summer before the season began, I was standing on the sidelines of an American football team practice at Howard. I was holding onto the fence, looking but not seeing, when a medical intern came up to me. "You look pensive, Coach," he said. I told him I was looking for a quotation for the team to rally behind. Easy, he said: "Truth, crushed to earth, shall rise again."

It was a line of verse from 19th century American poet William Cullen Bryant that had often been repeated by the Reverend Martin Luther King in his civil rights speeches. I, a lover of inspirational quotes, found it apt. "Truth," I muttered, "Truth . . ." The truth was that we were the best college team in the United States. The truth was that the forces of the NCAA had been arrayed against us ever since we'd humbled the soccer powerhouses. The truth was that we'd been crushed by an unfair interpretation of the rules, and we would rise again.

From the first day of pre-season training, it was our mantra.

Coach Chambers still traveled with the team although he had no real duties. He could still inspire. When we huddled and Coach belched out a prayer, you'd be ready to fight! Before the 1971 semi-final against Harvard, he told the assembled players: "Gentlemen, I never thought I would see in my lifetime the capstone of white education playing the capstone of black education." Then he broke down and cried. In his 70s, he was confined to a wheelchair, but when he chose to travel, the players hoisted him onto the bus like he was sitting in a palanquin.

The soccer in the 1974 regular season was hard. My recruiting had raised not only the level of Howard's game, but also compelled other coaches to look further afield for talent. Ibrahim Ibrahim, coach of Clemson University in South Carolina, wasn't shy about following the Tiger's tracks to look for game. Clemson was the big name in the South, and when we came up against them in 1971, they had had a lonesome black player. We beat up on them that year. The next year, I goggled at the dark-skinned Clemson players filing off the bus: "What happen to your players?" I heckled Ibrahim. "You paint them!" He had gone to Guyana to recruit. He also went to Jamaica after I did, and then Nigeria. Eventually, he simply snatched away my already-landed players.

A coach I did have a great deal of respect for was Harry Keough. Keough had worked for the U.S. Postal Service while playing professional soccer. He was a defender on the U.S. team that beat England 1-0 in the 1950 World Cup—a result that remains one of the most shocking upsets in the history of sport. In his time as coach of St Louis University, he won five NCAA championships. After my 1972 speech when I accused the NCAA of racism for declaring several players ineligible, he had claimed ignorance of the origin of the investigation. "Lincoln, I don't know what happened," he said. "You have to trust me. I am a soccer coach; I am coming out to beat you." I believed him. He played it fair and square.

I would soon have the chance to meet Keough again. The Howard University Bison soccer team was storming through to the 1974 NCAA Men's Soccer final. Harry Keough and St Louis University would be waiting.

The 1974 playoffs began with George Washington University. I still have a picture of my eight-year-old son Sheldon on the sideline, his mouth wide with amazement as a Howard player in the foreground puts a wicked dribble on an opposing player. George Washington had done their scouting, and neutralized us stubbornly. We won 2-0, but it hadn't been a walkover. Next, we met Clemson and coach Ibrahim, who had ditched his white players. We snuck past them 1-0 on a header by Dominic Ezeani.

The quarter-final found us matched up against our old brawling buddies, Philadelphia Textile. Before the match, reporters asked me: "If you were Walter Chyzowych (Philadelphia Textile coach), what would you do to beat your team?" I must have snorted. "What kind of question is that?" I said. "That's his problem."

It was bitterly cold. Cold enough that players' toenails blackened and fell off three days later. The referee took the match into his own hands, blatantly awarding penalties to Philadelphia. Pacing the sideline, focused on the game, I turned around to tell Nigerian national Sunny Izevbigie to warm up. All I saw was a row of eyes. The substitutes had found a blanket and were swaddled together in a little clump. Sunny whined: "Coach, it's too cold." His warm-up was the most desultory I've ever seen. He ran on, and immediately buried a left-footer. The score was 4-2. The ref gave Philadelphia one more penalty for good measure before the final whistle blew. He'd awarded them three, and we won 5-3.

Hartwick College came down from the Catskill Mountains in New York to meet us in the semi-final. Kendo Ilodigwe, who had a knack for spotting a goalie off his line, saw the Hartwick netminder near the edge of his area and, quick as a flash, toe-poked a long shot that arced over his head and settled in the net. We were off to meet St Louis in the final.

It was December in St Louis, Missouri, and Busch Stadium was blanketed in snow for the 1974 NCAA championship game. The warm locker room smelled of muscle rub and stale sweat. Around the room, each player tended to his pre-game ritual—rubbing himself down, listening to reggae, strapping his strappable parts. I gave them a talk and we warmed up as a group. We were used to saying the prayer and then running straight out of the locker room and onto the field. If the door didn't open, we'd have burst a hole through the wall!

Just after the prayer, the referee came in: "Coach, it'll take half an hour to clear the snow." Tractors were muscling the snow into great mounds around the field. We were forced to sit, and the room went silent. What more could I say? Then, one of the Africans chanted something in a language I didn't understand. From the other side of the room, someone responded in a baritone. Back and forth the chants went, and it was heavy. It could have been the fortifying lament of Africans in the bowels of the slave ships.

Jamaican national half-back Paul Pringle pulled a pair of small skulls from his bag and walked around, holding them up in front of each player and repeating ominously: "Skulls! Skulls!"

Finally, an official returned and told us the field was ready.

Before match day, I had found myself with a goalkeeping dilemma. Eritrean, Amdemichael Selassie, was calm and very competent. Trinidadian, Trevor Leiba, was flashy and flamboyant. Selassie had two points in his favour. Firstly, he was in his final year, while Leiba was a freshman. In American college sports, all other things being equal, the senior should get the opportunity to start. Secondly, according to the roster, it was Selassie's turn to play. At the beginning of the season, I'd decided I didn't want either keeper sitting on the bench to rot, so I'd told them that they'd alternate, one match on and one match off. "You all make the decision who plays first." So it had gone for the entire season, up to the semi-final where Leiba had saved very well in our 2-1 victory over Hartwick College.

The night before the final, I was restless. According to the run of things, Selassie was the man. Yet, I had a nagging feeling in my gut. Something was saying, "Ay, Gut: Don't do that." Perhaps it was the ghost of Billy Jones. Jones was the keeper I'd decided to stick with in the 1970 semi-final. Nursing an injury and possibly traumatized by an on-field brawl, he had lost us the match.

At the pre-game meeting in the hotel, I tacked the team starting list to the wall. When Leiba saw his name, he looked over at Selassie, who shrugged. Selassie felt that I'd favoured a countryman. He was very upset, and he had every reason to be. I had gone back on my word.

She was so pregnant with our last son Derek that her stomach touched the steering wheel when she pulled up in our canary yellow Mustang. I had told her not to drive all the way to St Louis! Obviously, she hadn't listened. Wild horses couldn't keep me away, said my wife, and smiled so sweetly that I melted. At least her father had insisted that she put snow-tires on the car for the long journey from our home in Maryland. She had also brought two of the players' girlfriends to share the drive.

St Louis played Barcelona-style soccer—very possessive with lots of close passing. They probed constantly until they found a gap to exploit. We were deadly on the counter-attack—pass, pass, off to the races. But the contrasting styles had nothing to do with our slow start in that 1974 final; nor can I blame the slippery pitch. We were a step behind from the opening whistle. Ian Bain was having an uncharacteristically terrible game in midfield, mistiming balls in the air and failing to complete his passes. We had no feel for the Astroturf, and by the half we were down 1-0.

In the dressing room, I needed to make a change in midfield to swing the momentum. I turned to central defender Dominic Ezeani. "Dom, we need you to straighten out the half-line," I said, and instructed him to play central midfield. "I not moving," he said, which totally befuddled me. Ezeani had played midfield for Nigeria, but had accepted a defensive role at Howard. "All year round," he continued, "I am playing out of my position. Coach, I am not moving."

I had three other midfield options. One was All-Nigerian Sunny Izevbigie; the second was Jamaican national half-back Paul Pringle, carrier of motivational skulls; and the third was Miyiwa Sanya. (General Barnaby Tulloch was injured.) For some reason, I turned to Mario Mc Lennan, a defender. Mario was one of the Jamaican schoolboys who I'd picked up on the 1972 tour. He hadn't played much for the entire season. He was arrogant and unfit, and so skilful that he gave me heart palpitations by dribbling opponents in no-beat zones. His nickname was "Skill." "Mario," I said, "I want you to play half-back." Sunny looked at me with a stare colder than the Busch Stadium turf.

The first thing Mario did in the second half was put the ball through a St Louis player's legs. Then he collected a pass and returned it for a neat one-two in a tiny space. Mario's match-fitness was so low that he couldn't sustain that level for more than fifteen minutes, but by the time I pulled him off, the momentum had swung. Early in the second half, winger Balotunde Balogun took the ball to the right side of the field and twice faked a cross, causing the defender to slide off the pitch and into the snowbank. As the defender came back, looking like the Abominable Snowman, Tunde beat him again and crossed with his right. Yomi Bamiro headed it in. It stayed 1-1 until the whistle blew to end regulation time.

Somewhere in Busch Stadium that day, there was a sign. There is dispute about what it said, and whether it came across the official electronic scoreboard or was just a placard carried by a fan. It read: "The monkeys are here!" or "See the monkeys dance!" or something about gorillas playing soccer. No one seems to remember clearly. Perhaps we partially blocked it from our memories. Maybe we just had more important things to do that day than fret about bigotry.

We went four overtime periods. Twice we hit the woodwork but didn't score. Then, Real Kill Davy got the ball between two St Louis defenders on the left side. They thought they had him, until he pushed in an extra gear, blew past them, and whipped a deadly ball across the icy field. Through the goalkeeper's hands went the icy orb, falling between several players from both sides. Kendo Ilodigwe, who adored his gifted World Cup '74 boots, was the first to get to it. It was no more than a toe, but the ball flew into the goal.

Before it had even settled, Kendo was off and running, his arms extended like wings. Man, we cried! Ian Bain, one of only two players still around from the stripped 1971 championship could only muster: "You know how long I've played for this . . ." Keith Look Loy shed his shirt, ran through the frigid air, and jumped on top of me. "We win! We win! We win!" Then he darted off into the stands.

Who knew what the chanting had meant, or Pringle's skulls? Where had they come from? Was there any difference between his macabre charms and a Westerner's rabbit foot?

We had not lost a game for the season. People kept thinking we were flukes, and we'd kept on winning. For the *second* time, we'd become the first African-American college to win an NCAA championship. Truth, I tell you. Truth. Nothing but the truth.

The 1974 team has kept in contact; some more assiduously than others. Despite the jubilation, there were a couple who felt aggrieved. When it was time to take the team photograph, Mario Mc Lennan, benched for much of the season, wanted nothing to do with it. At our 25th anniversary reunion, he cried. Skill was still disappointed that he hadn't played a larger role. But he hadn't stood where I had, and seen the crucial effect of his presence on the game. Things happen like that sometimes. You can be so absorbed in doing your job that you have no idea of your place in history. "You were the man," I assured him. "It started from you." Mario had mashed up the place for fifteen minutes, and turned the game around.

A couple years after the final, Selassie built up the courage to ask about my decision to put Trevor Leiba in net. "Coach, why did you do that?" he said. "Trevor had three years to go." I really couldn't answer. Eventually, I said, "The decision was made in my gut." Selassie later said that winning was the main thing, and you respect the coach's decision, whatever it may be.

Hundreds of students, faculty members, and administration officials jammed the Cramton Auditorium at Howard for a celebration after our win. A DJ announced each player's name as he accepted his medal. Kendo, our match winner, was dressed in red pants, a red shirt, and a pair of red shoes. "FIIIIRE!!!" bellowed the DJ. The *Washington Post* had asked him immediately after he netted the championship-winning goal what he would have done if he hadn't scored. In typically melodramatic fashion, he said he would have died.

T&T pioneers in the fledgling North American Soccer League, 1968. (L to R) Jan Steadman and Leroy De Leon of the New York Generals, Lincoln Phillips of the Baltimore Bays, and Warren Archibald of the Generals.

I get the better of Pelé (for once) in a game between the Baltimore Bays and Santos of Brazil.

Holding on, as player/coach for the Washington Darts.

Darts, winners of the International Trophy 1970, stacked with
T&T nationals: (Back row) Bertram Grell (third from left), Victor
Gamaldo (fourth from left), Leroy De Leon (fifth from left), Me (#1
jersey), Selris Figaro (second from right). (Front row) Winston Alexis
(left), Gerry Brown (third from right), Warren Archibald (right).

Two of the Darts' best defenders—Victor Gamaldo (R)
and Willie Evans—double up to mark Pelé.

A sizzling shot brings out the best in me while keeping for the Darts.

Howard Bisons—NCAA champions, 1971.

Linda and baby Derek share my accomplishment—a Bachelor of Science degree from Howard University.

Celebrating the 1971 NCAA championship with Coach Chambers.

The 1974 Howard Bisons—still the only U.S. college team ever to win a national championship untied and unbeaten.

O 0110482 JAN 10 2074
FM SECSTATE WASHDC
TO AMEMBASSY KINGSTON IMMEDIATE 5208
BT
UNCLAS STATE 000005

EMBASSY REQUESTED TO PASS FOLLOWING MESSAGE FROM
PRESIDENT NIXON TO HOWARD UNIVERSITY COACH LINCOLN
PHILLIPS, C/O GODFREY BEDFORD, PHONE 938-0342, STAYING
ON UNIVSERSITY OF JAMAICA CAMPUS:

BEGIN TEXT: MY HEARTIEST CONGRATULATIONS TO YOU AND
THE HOWARD UNIVESITY SOCCER TEAM. YR TEAM. YOUR
VICTORY YESTERDAY, THE PERFECT SEASON OF FIFTEEN
WINS AND NO LOSSES, AND YOUR NCAA
CHAMPIONSHIP MAKE ALL WASHINGTON VERY PROUD.

YOU HAVE MADE A GREAT SEASON FOR WASHINGTON TEAMS EVEN
BETTER.

GOOD LUCK IN YOUR EXHIBITION GAMES IN THE WEST
INDIES. WASHINGTON LOOKS FORWARD TO THE RETURN OF ITS
CHAMPION.

                    SIGNED

                    RICHARD NIXON

END TEXT

THE WHITE HOUSE
WASHINGTON

December 16, 1974

Dear Coach Phillips:

I want to extend to you and to your fine
Bison soccer team my heartiest congratu-
lations for winning the 1974 NCAA Soccer
Championship.

Your hard-fought victory in the fourth
overtime period in St. Louis was a very
exciting victory and a fitting climax to a
highly successful season. You have
brought great pride to Howard University
and to the entire Capital area, and I want
to commend you and all of the team members on your achievement.

With my warm best wishes.

Sincerely,

Gerald R. Ford

Mr. Lincoln Phillips
Coach
Bison Soccer Team
Howard University
Washington, D. C.

Congratulations from presidents Ford and Nixon; Bermudan
Stan Smith, captain of the 1971 championship team.

Howard All-Americans, Keith Aqui and the airborne Alvin Henderson.

Winston "Rick" Yallery-Arthur celebrates the 1971 championship after overcoming tremendous health issues.

Donnie Simmons of Bermuda.

A driving force for the Bisons—Howard administrator Dr. Carl Anderson, with Pelé at a Howard training clinic.

Nigerian Sunny Izevbigie played a major role in taking us to the 1974 title.

The Davy brothers from Jamaica— (From left) Richard "Real Kill", Mikey, and Kenneth "Dirty Harry."

Ian Bain and Tony Martin (Howard sweater)—the only two
men to play on both the '71 and '74 championship teams.

Keith "Barnaby" Tulloch from Jamaica—one of the
most productive half-backs in Howard history.

"Shoot!" My son Sheldon urges Nigerian Miyiwa Sanya to have a crack in a game against George Washington University in 1974.

Gooooool!!! Sanya celebrates.

12—HOME AGAIN, HOME AGAIN

Port-of-Spain, Trinidad
2004

From a shack in St James, Trinidad, I'd traveled further than I could ever have dreamed. I'd spent almost forty years in the United States, playing professional soccer and coaching everyone from the physically disabled to the best college team in the country. I had plumbed the depths of despair, and celebrated triumph. Now, in 2004, it was time to go back home.

Before this story sours, I want to tell you: I had no delusions. I was hopeful, yes, but clear-eyed. I had been looking for an opportunity to play a role in Trinidad and Tobago football for years; it had just never worked out. Until Jack Warner came knocking.

A black man from a small island, risen to the top of the governing body of the world's most popular and lucrative sport! Jack Warner— FIFA vice-president, power-broker, king-maker, dictator. Always surrounded by scandal; never proven guilty. Jack had built the Trinidad and Tobago Football Federation (T&TFF) around him, and everyone within the organization knew who they owed their jobs to. Absolute loyalty kept you at work.

So Jack calls and asks me to come see him at the Concacaf (Confederation of North, Central American and Caribbean Association Football) office in New York. He is also president of Concacaf and he controls the entire region's vote at FIFA. (If you know anything about FIFA, you can guess at the value of this.) I am speaking to a savvy man. "Tiger, I feel we have a good chance to qualify for the World Cup (in Germany, 2006)," says Jack. "But I can't do it by myself. All of us have our talents in different areas and we must combine those talents."

The T&TFF was on the verge of dismissing Tobagonian Bertille St Clair as coach of the national team, and I had been promised the job. I felt Bertille had done well enough and the team results at the region's Gold Cup didn't justify his sacking. As snow fell outside the window, Jack ploughed on: "You're a foreigner, but you're also a local. You have a winning record; everything you touch, succeeds." I admit I was enjoying the flattery. "Besides that, everybody likes you. You would be the one to bring some credibility to the football program."

Jack was right: The T&TFF had an image problem. Mostly because of Jack himself. He had been implicated in more than one ticket-selling scandal for FIFA events, although nothing has ever been proven in court. My image, at least with the generation who remembered my play, was stellar.

Jon Stueckenschneider was a New York City cop. He had also been my assistant for a couple years when I coached Virginia Commonwealth University (VCU) after leaving Howard. Stueck was a big-city, white American who had spent so much time around Trinis on the VCU team that we had granted him honorary T&T citizenship. He loved to roll out his terrible sing-song imitation of the Trini accent.

On uniform patrol in Spanish Harlem, Upper Manhattan one night, Stueck came upon a collision between a NYC cab and a very nice Jaguar. The cab hardly had a scratch and the driver was sent on his way after protesting that he had a fare. The Jag meanwhile, was worse for wear, and the driver hung his head dejectedly.

"Have you been drinking?" asked Stueck, as he checked out the red, white and black national flag hanging from the rearview mirror. The driver refused to answer. Stueck tried another approach: "Where you from?" "Trinidad," responded the driver. "Oh Gawd!" burst Stueck in his worst imitation of a Trini accent, "so am I. You like football?" The man responded that he did indeed like football. "Well, I going to ask you a question," continued the cop, "and I'll lock you up if you answer wrong." Hardly expecting to play a game show when he'd left home that evening, the driver gripped his steering wheel tightly. "Who's the greatest man ever save[37] for Trinidad?" Thinking hard, the contestant bent his head. When he came up, he answered tentatively: "Lincoln Phillips." Stueck sent him into the Harlem night with an: "Oh Gawd, that's the answer! Sir, have a good night."

Two thousand miles from home, the memory of my days as a top-flight goalkeeper was still intact.

But I didn't want the job of coach as Jack had suggested. My competitive fire no longer burned as hot; I felt the position should be filled by a younger man. I proposed that they divide the job of coach/technical director into two positions. I would be happy to be technical director, responsible for football development, while Bertille held on to his job as coach (at least temporarily). I had experience as a technical director for a very large youth soccer club in Maryland.

Linda and I sold our furniture, locked up our house in Maryland, and headed off to Trinidad. Sheldon, my eldest son who is also a lawyer, drew up a contract that included very precise job requirements. We felt there should be standards by which I could be measured. For the first year, Jack paid my salary directly. I was sixty-three.

Not long into my stay in Trinidad, I traveled with the national team to England for a couple warm-up matches. We did not play particularly well, and coach Bertille's day of reckoning drew closer. Bertille was a disciplinarian, and one of the few coaches who looked out for the welfare of each and every one of his players, but his recent results had not been good. He knew that Jack and the T&TFF had been looking for a replacement.

It was then that I first reached out to Dutch coach, Leo Beenhakker.

I had become intrigued by the Dutch system of player development at the Chesapeake Dragons—a club that my son Sheldon and I had formed to groom youngsters for entry into American pro-soccer. I knew the Dutch started their youngsters on football fundamentals early, and I felt the approach was sorely needed in Trinidad, where it wasn't unusual to find senior footballers who weren't much good at holding on to the ball. I never had the chance to go Dutch at Chesapeake (the club floundered for lack of financing

---

[37]   Goalkeep.

and a training facility), but I did learn the name of Dutchman Leo Beenhakker.

With Bertille on the way out, Sheldon called and told me that "Don Leo"—who had coached the Netherlands, Real Madrid, and championship-winning Dutch clubs such as Ajax—might be open to a chat about coaching in T&T. I called. We began discussions about him coming to coach youth clinics, but the conversation soon turned to the possibility of trying to get the national team into the World Cup. "What are the chances?" asked Beenhakker. "Very slim," I responded honestly, "but we could make it."

Twice I mentioned Beenhakker to Jack; on the second, I was soundly rebuffed. "I don't want to hear anything more about it," he ordered. "I have enquired about this Beenhakker, and FIFA doesn't like him. I am going by two hundred years' experience (FIFA's history). And besides, I have somebody else."

Ron Atkinson had coached some big-name, first division English clubs, including Manchester United and Aston Villa, before moving on to TV football commentary. "Big Ron" as he was known, tumbled ingloriously from the media after saying in front of an open mic that Chelsea player Marcel Desailly was "what is known in some schools as a #@&!*@# lazy n—." He'd been out of coaching since 1999. This is the man Jack Warner wanted to hire to coach the Trinidad and Tobago Soca Warriors in 2004.

Jack waded right into a mutiny. With the national team assembled, he announced that Atkinson was the likely pick to replace Tobagonian Bertille St Clair. He turned to former Aston Villa and Manchester United striker Dwight Yorke for support. "Is Ron a good coach?" asked Jack. "Absolutely," said Dwight, "but he's a #@&!*@# racist." Goalkeeper Shaka Hislop, who had played for Newcastle and West Ham United, and once suffered racist taunts from his very own fans, was adamant: He wouldn't be part of any team coached by Atkinson. Shaka, who by then had supported British educational charity "Show Racism the Red Card" for almost a decade, said he felt that "it would have reflected poorly on him to be part of that charade." With the two biggest names on the team stridently opposed to his pick, Jack jammed it in reverse and peeled rubber. "It's not written in stone," he said. "We just had some preliminary discussions."

The players also made it clear that while some of them played in England, they weren't great fans of the English style. Asked what style he preferred, Dwight said Dutch. Ever the astute politician, Jack adjusted quickly: "What if I told you Leo Beenhakker was on our short-list." After the meeting, he instructed me to begin negotiations with Beenhakker.

We started well enough, the "Don" and I. He came with a raft of assistants, and all he wanted was a little advice on what he should say to the foreign-based professional players. I readily obliged. But as we went along, the tension between us mounted. He had taken a history-making job with little time on the clock. *If* we qualified—and that was a remote possibility considering that we only had one point from three matches—we'd be the smallest nation ever to get to a World Cup. Beenhakker took the job on the simple condition that he be given absolute freedom to do as he saw fit.

It was hard for me not to be seen as meddling. As a local, and hero of yesteryear, I shared a relationship with some of the players that the Dutchman could not. When striker Stern John couldn't hit a goal the size of a barn, I gave him some picong about just how dreadful he was, before I boosted him back up. "Just now you go start scoring," I said, "you are a streak player." Before a match against Guatemala, I prayed with Stern and captain Russell Latapy, asking God to bless their feet. I had Shaka Hislop stand on tennis balls to improve his balance and enjoyed talking goalkeeping with him after a training camp in England. All the players came to chat. Perhaps this made Beenhakker uneasy. Not even his coaching assistants dared open their mouths at half-time.

The media also approached me for my opinions from time to time. I thought I was careful not to contradict the coach, or talk tactics with players, but it was inevitable that we'd butt heads. The first clash came after I spoke to the press about Beenhakker's exclusion of a defender who I felt should have made the squad. The guy wasn't very fast, but you couldn't run past him. When the press asked what I thought, I simply said, "Well, that's what the coach wants." It ticked Beenhakker off. He called me into a meeting, with the football federation's press liaison present. "Any comments to the press about my team," said the silver-haired Don, "must come from me only." He warned that as technical director, I was to say nothing about the team.

Although Beenhakker later dismissed my concern, I felt that I made another mistake by asking him to have a look at my youngest son, Derek, a talented defender who had played semi-professionally in the United States and at third division level in Ireland and Germany. Derek had played two matches for the national team under Bertille, who was trying to find the right players for a World Cup run. In his first, against South Korea, he had a good game. Despite cramping badly in the muggy conditions, he stuck it out to the final whistle to see his team earn a 1-1 draw. But in his second match in national colours, he was injured. It took a while to diagnose him, his rehab wasn't good, and he didn't heal well.

By the time Beenhakker arrived, Derek wasn't really enjoying life in Trinidad. Like all my sons, he was born in Trinidad but raised in America, and was finding it hard fitting in. Playing a practice match in front of the Don, he ran awkwardly, and a ball ricocheted off his foot straight to an opponent. I felt the coach might no longer trust my judgment. But Beenhakker was generous enough to say that the favour I had asked was a "very normal request from a father."

Meanwhile, Jack Warner was managing both Beenhakker and me by ensuring that we conferred only with him on any decision of consequence. He was a little autocrat who made it clear that other members of the football federation executive were to be ignored. In the beginning, Warner paid my salary from his own pocket; he was the piper and I followed his tune, to an extent.

I enjoyed interacting with the national players. I understood the humble backgrounds many of them came from and the mentorship they may have lacked. I always cracked jokes around them and observed their moods and attitudes, ready to step in with advice or counsel if I felt it was needed.

I sometimes worry about the lack of mentors in T&T today. For me, there was Pa Aleong with his bike and bench, scheduling training sessions to sort out any weakness; and Georgie, my paternal half-brother who took the time to show me how to shoot a basketball properly. There was Joey Gonsalves, a national sporting hero in his own right, who generously critiqued and complimented my play on the football field. They made me not just a better player but a better person.

Throughout my coaching career, I was always guided by a principle: The game isn't just a game; it can shape people. It's no good being strong and capable on the soccer field if it doesn't transfer to your life. If I can do for others a quarter of what my mentors did for me, my life would have been worthwhile.

The T&T fans who went to the Germany World Cup in 2006 were vocal and patriotic. They swathed themselves in red, white and black, and partied hard. Everyone loved the story of the smallest ever World Cup qualifier, which now had a shot at toppling giants. For our debut World Cup match against heavily-favoured Sweden, I was in the stands, watching as our first string goalkeeper Kelvin Jack warmed up. He didn't look sharp at all, and I had no idea that he'd strained his calf. Coach Beenhakker only told Shaka Hislop that he was going to start ten minutes before the match. The Don considered Shaka the number three goalie.

According to Shaka, the last-minute notice was a blessing in disguise. He had always been a nervous starter, and in this, a huge game on the biggest stage, he might have been a bundle of nerves. The day of that match, he had a lovely breakfast and a relaxing morning before he was thrust into the lion's mouth. As the team walked out, I noticed the change: "Wait a minute; that's Shaka!" They played the national anthem, and my hair stood on end. Beside me, a tough guy named Baldy, who had been around football for a long time, cried long tears. "Tiger, boy, it just get to me."

Shaka made some wonderful saves, including one off a thumping volley by Zlatan Ibrahimovic, and T&T defended stoutly with ten men for the entire second half after one of our defenders was sent off. Beenhakker's master tactics, based on his assessment of the Sweden coach's conservative nature, helped us to a 0-0 draw. The result thrilled an entire nation. (Us; not the Swedes.) Although we lost 2-0 to both Paraguay and England and failed to advance past the first round, we weren't easily outclassed.

Back in Trinidad, my duties were being taken away for political reasons until I was left with a single major responsibility: Preparing coaches for entry-level 'D-license' coaching certification. This was going well. I had certified eight hundred D-license coaches all over the country. We did courses in Blanchisseuse, Couva, Princes Town, San

Fernando, and many places in between. The courses were necessary because the coaches were learning to teach the most basic skills—trapping, dribbling, and passing—all of which were technically flawed at the highest level. It was good to see coaches who had previously yelled and cursed their players, transformed from: "Ay, boy, you kicking the ball over bars!" to: "You need to get over the ball, like this."

The most enjoyable coaching sessions took place behind the razor wire and chain link fence of the Golden Grove prison, in the "Reform through Football" program. There I met Michael "Fires" Haughey, a man who had earned his nickname by setting people ablaze. During the orientation, Haughey slouched in his chair tapping his fingers. "Inmates," said the guard, "You have a good opportunity, so listen to Mr. Phillips." Haughey tapped away. When my turn came, I looked at the twenty felons seated before me, took a deep breath, and began: "Gentlemen, I heard every time your names were called, you were mentioned as inmates. To me, you are not inmates; you are fellow coaches." Haughey sat up. Aha, I said to myself, I got you.

The prisoners enjoyed themselves thoroughly, playing outdoors and learning the rudiments of coaching. They studied late into the night to pass their written test, helped by the prison guards who had taken the course before them. When the session ended, there were about six votes of thanks. At the podium, convict Adrian Gokool said: "I do plenty bad things, and I doh expect to come out of here. Before this course, I doh care if I die. If I ever come out of here, I going to do something with a ball. But if I doh come out, I go help the younger prisoners." He was voted MVP—Most Valuable Prisoner—and I cried as he shed a tear. The new coaches agreed that the course had helped them see the guards in a different light.

But Trinidad had changed since I left in the late 1960s, and the prison course is one of the last good memories of my return home. While Linda and I had been put up in a very nice house in Maraval where we enjoyed entertaining, we were alarmed by the erosion of middle class values. Crime had increased, and so had apathy. The politics of football was lethal.

The People's National Movement (PNM) was in government, and Jack Warner belonged at the time to the opposition United National Congress (UNC). He had no problem using football as his pawn in a giant chess match that was ultimately about politics. At first, he praised my four-year, TT $29 million plan (about US $4.5 million) for the development of football for boys and girls. "Tiger, this is the best thing I have ever seen," said Warner when the plan was presented.

It was indeed a solid piece of research. The plan, geared towards producing elite footballers on a regular basis, was comprehensive— from the community up to the leagues. It envisioned youth teams from the Under-14 level on up, traveling to the United States to compete in tournaments annually. The practice sessions for these youth teams were itemized down to the last cent—so many dollars in taxi fares, so much money for the kids to eat, so much for ice and drinks. It laid the groundwork for the establishment of a high-performance football academy at the Ato Boldon Stadium.

I had defended the coaching development program like a thesis in front of two former Howard University players who had gone on to work at the university, and honed it by adding elements from the Australian sporting academies—one of the world's most successful systems for identifying and nurturing athletes.

The Sport Company approved the plan and so did the Ministry of Sport. Warner said it was wonderful, and then abruptly changed his mind. The T&T Football Federation (Warner's fiefdom) also withdrew its support. Instead of being promoted as a Trinidad and Tobago Football Federation proposal, the plan was suddenly strung up and mocked as the sole work of Lincoln Phillips. Some believed that Warner was afraid of making the PNM look good. Maybe he predicted that it would affect his almost total control of the sport. Government had pledged to fund the program, which would have diminished his sway. My plan was shelved.

The loss of the development plan stung, but the ruination of a personal relationship hurt much more.

The last thing Keith Look Loy's mother told me before I took her boy child to play football in a school far far away was: "Take care of my son." I took this very seriously. Never mind that I made the poor boy look like a sheep that had been shorn with a pair of garden shears when I cut his Afro. He, of all my players, recognized that the Howard drive for dominance was an ideological battle. The wars of liberation in Africa, the shabby treatment we received in an Anglo-dominated sport, Marxist-Leninist ideology—it all contributed to his militant,

Afro-conscious sensibility. He was a good football player, but he was also an ideal candidate for spontaneous combustion.

Keith once hurt himself in the pre-season, so I kept him off the field, afraid that he'd be re-injured with one well-aimed kick. Playing a tight game against Davis & Elkins College, however, I decided to bring him off the bench just after half-time. Turning around, I couldn't find Keith. Peeved that he hadn't been put on at the half, he had abandoned the bench and walked up into the stands. I suspended him for two games, but ordered him to accompany the team on our next road trip even though he wouldn't dress.

I was destined to encounter Keith in Trinidad, decades after he'd played a role in winning the 1974 championship for Howard University. Jack Warner had tired of Keith's constant, eloquent letters-to-the-editor decrying Warner's management of local football, so he shut him up by giving him a job. The letters stopped, but Warner now had a human resource problem in the form of a passionate, opinionated man who often rubbed people the wrong way. He shuffled Keith around from job to job until he ended up directly under me, as technical adviser to the technical director.

We would clash over girls.

T&T was going to host the Under-17 Women's World Cup in 2010. Jack was insistent that our girls should qualify for the preceding World Cup, in New Zealand 2008, to gain experience that would allow us to put in a decent performance on home turf. Women's football in T&T wasn't nearly as popular as it is in much of the developed world, so forming a competitive team wasn't going to be easy. Especially with just three months on the clock. Luckily, I had a top-class American contact.

Randy Waldrum is one of the best women's coaches in the United States. In twenty-two seasons of coaching in the ultra-competitive US women's college leagues, he has won 370 games and lost only ninety-four. His Notre Dame University team has twice won the national championship, and when they haven't won it all, they've been near the top. He's since gone on to become head coach of the U.S. Women's Under-23 team. Randy and I worked together in the 1990s, training coaches for the U.S. Soccer Federation, and he had since called on me as a specialist goalkeeping coach for his summer camp at Baylor

University. If anyone could qualify the local girls on short notice, it was him.

Randy blew Jack's mind and was able to quickly negotiate a three-month contract. He appreciated the girls' desire to learn, but he recognized that T&T wasn't going to qualify for the World Cup. The girls were small, lacked technical ability because they'd been introduced to football later than their opponents, and weren't fit enough. There was a tiny ray of hope: Girls of T&T parentage living in North America. There were enough of them, of sufficient quality, to justify a camp in Florida where we could compare the local girls to the "foreigners." The mere suggestion stirred up the local cartel. The swarm of opposition was led by none other than Keith Look Loy.

He immediately said that he didn't want any foreign-based players. Perhaps it should have been no surprise, since his attitude to America had always been ambivalent. He may have seen it as denying the local girls opportunity, or considered it an imperialist intervention. He referred to Randy as my "friend" rather than a pedigreed women's coach and claimed that Randy only wanted to use the foreign-based girls rather than choosing the team by merit. Keith was supported by local women's coaches who weren't happy about ceding control to any foreigner. In the background, Jack was telling Randy to do whatever he had to in order to qualify, but Keith was contradicting his boss by opposing Randy's every move. A mix of foreign-based and local girls eventually acquitted themselves well, failing to qualify for the World Cup by the slimmest of margins—goal difference.

Jack seemed pleased with the local girls' performance but Keith deemed it a total failure. Maneuvering behind Jack's back, Keith won the day. Randy was flushed away, along with our plans for the development of women's football starting with an academy system. A new women's coach, who couldn't hold a candle to Randy, was appointed. His performance since can only be described as dismal.

This was the beginning of Keith's open disapproval of my methods. From then on, he won most battles and was instrumental in sidelining me completely. He refers to this incident as a "philosophical departure," but his behaviour hurt both me, and, I believe, the development of women's football. What was most distressing was that he allowed himself to be used to encroach on responsibilities that were clearly under my purview.

"By the time we got to this, because of these political battles, there was a bit of distance between Lincoln and myself. But I never stopped respecting him and being grateful for what he did for me. By giving me a scholarship to Howard, he shaped the rest of my life."

Keith Look Loy—Howard University player, T&TFF technical adviser

"Lincoln fought Keith as if he was a real enemy. I didn't think he truly was. It was a difference of philosophy. I said, 'Lincoln, you are the one who taught us to be independent in thought about the game. And now you're angry because he doesn't think like you! You were his mentor.'"

Alvin Henderson—Howard University player, T&TFF technical committee

"Keith Look Loy didn't grasp, nor want to grasp the whole picture. The development plan was well thought-out: Let's work on the here and now, but in the meantime let's start to develop the talent pool so we're better prepared for the next World Cup. I never understood his opposition."

Randy Waldrum—women's coach

Yet the roots run deep with Keith. And the soil of my hurt is too thin for a grudge to flourish.

After the men's World Cup of 2006, Leo Beenhakker's assistant Wim Rijsbergen took over as coach of the T&T men's team. The Dutchman was patronizing, so he had few friends among the players. He had even fewer friends in the T&TFF because he openly criticized the administration. Some of his critiques were fair, but his Dutch bluntness wasn't appreciated.

He stormed into my office one day, hot and bothered, waving a newspaper article in which I had commented to the press about a standoff between Jack and the national team. Jack had reneged on a promise to pay the players bonuses after the World Cup, and the more insistent players had been blacklisted from the national team. I had told the media that we had to put the situation behind us because the opposition doesn't care about internal turmoil; they just want to kick our butts. Rijsbergen was furious. He loomed over my chair, shoving the article in my face. "Lincoln, I don't want you to say anything to the papers about the players!" he shouted. "It's my team!" I got the impression that he wanted to fight.

I stood so we were nose to nose. Red-faced Rijsbergen roared on, cursing about 'effin this and 'effin that! I shoved him in his chest, he stumbled backwards, and came charging back. The second time, I chucked him in his neck, hard, and he retreated down the stairs. I sat at my desk, my heart thumping. I was angry beyond belief.

We were both summoned, to appear separately before a hearing of the T&TFF disciplinary committee. I admitted that I had initiated the physical confrontation, but said I'd only done so because he had violated my space. "I'm a soldier," I said. "I know how to defend my space." Rijsbergen also had his say. I was told that he couldn't control himself, and insulted a panel member. "You people . . ." he blurted, clearly on the verge of losing his cool. It was all they needed. He was suspended for six months before being replaced.

"No matter that Lincoln was instrumental, and one of the people responsible for bringing Beenhakker there—they (Beenhakker's coaching staff) didn't have the required respect for him. He's a good coach, with a resumé as long as the airport. But I realized that these guys couldn't see this proud black man being their technical director."

David Nakhid, former national player and assistant coach

It was in Bahrain, a wealthy little kingdom in the Middle East, that I first realized just how treacherous the earth beneath me was. A little gang, armed with shovels and picks, was working steadily to undermine me.

We'd gone to Bahrain to play a do-or-die match. The winner would advance to the 2006 World Cup less than a year later. As technical director, one of the most senior administrative positions in T&T football, I assumed I'd stay with the team. Beenhakker had other ideas. He kept me out of the hotel. To be fair, only the team and the coaching staff were allowed to stay there. Beenhakker said he always worked the same way, and to allow others in was to invite distraction.

When we won 1-0 (and the Bahraini supporters rained bottles and chairs onto the pitch) I was torn. I was overjoyed for the team, but sad for myself. I was less than two years into my job and already losing my footing. In a very sneaky way, they had started taking little things away from me. They took away so much that down the road, they could say that I wasn't doing anything, and be justified in firing me.

On returning to Trinidad after Bahrain, everyone was a boss, and everyone gave a congratulatory speech at the airport. I was not invited to sit among the stars, and I couldn't bring myself to be festive. Linda read my mood and signaled: Let's get out of here. The team traveled to the capital in a motorcade. My wife and I drove together. The mood in our car was somber.

13—ANYWHERE'S BETTER

Howard University, Washington DC
1975

Ibrahim Ibrahim didn't mind bending the rules. The coach of Clemson University had no qualms about waiting for one of my star Howard players outside of the gym to give him "some incentives" to defect to Clemson. The player he poached was the scorer of the 1974 championship-winning goal, Kendo Ilodigwe.

To the best of my Nigerian players' knowledge, I was the first American coach to get to Nigeria. But after the success of the 1974 team, Clemson and San Francisco went and found about six Nigerians each. Everyone stepped up their games, making NCAA men's soccer more competitive than it had ever been. Other teams began scouting talent-rich Europe. In 1975, we lost in the national semi-finals; in '76, we bowed out to Clemson (and Kendo Ilodigwe) in the quarters; and in 1977, things fell apart.

I had found Sylvanus Oriakhi at a college in Colorado. He was the hardest accurate kicker of the ball I had ever seen. As our leading goalscorer, he played a major role in getting us to a 21-1 record in 1977. But on the eve of the first-round playoff game against Appalachia State, Howard University athletics director Leo Miles realized that Oriakhi was a college transfer. According to NCAA rules, he should have sat out the year. Miles told the Howard *Hilltop*: "I had to respond in a responsible manner since I am the administrator. I had certified the player as being eligible and when I found out about the player, I had to call the NCAA to make a correction." He hoped to soften the NCAA's inevitable punishment by notifying them, but the authorities dropped the hammer hard. We had to forfeit all our games in 1977 *and* were suspended from postseason play for 1978 and 1979. It was the maximum possible penalty.

It was the second time we'd been found guilty of eligibility violations; the first being in 1971 when we were stripped of the title. What can I say in my own defence? I had been left to interpret a welter of sometimes vague NCAA rules, and I made a mistake. Oriakhi had only been at the Colorado college for a few weeks and he hadn't played any sport there. It said on his transcript that he was a new student, but technically he was a transfer. I expressed my frustration to the *Hilltop*: "It's just that it's so easy to break a rule. We have always had a NCAA representative on campus taking a look at the basketball, football and soccer teams. It got so bad at one time that we had to ask them to leave. They wouldn't be investigating anything specific, but just snooping around, and if they looked long enough they would be bound to find something. You can sneeze and break one of their rules."

The entire Howard administration, including one of the soccer team's boosters, Vice-president of Student Affairs Dr. Carl Anderson, was very upset. Leo Miles was furious. But there was still a feeling in some quarters that the NCAA was not enforcing its rules evenhandedly. After Howard's American football team was suspended from postseason play for a year in 1978, Anderson asked: "How do you smoke out racist attitudes? I've dealt with these people (the NCAA) since 1971 and I've seen too many inconsistencies. The athletic powers have been reprimanded but the smaller schools have been given penalties."

Today, the NCAA Eligibility Center researches the eligibility of each and every player before he or she can play. It reduces the chances of an ineligible player getting on the field to almost zero.

In 1980, we were back from suspension. Oriakhi, my #10, was co-captain with Jamaican Bancroft Gordon. He was raring to go. "For me, it is a year of revenge," Oriakhi told the *Hilltop*, "because I felt I was victimized by my suspension." I told the paper I was "cautiously optimistic" about a repeat of 1974, when we'd won the national title after coming off a similar suspension from post-season play.

We won nine games for the 1980 season, and lost only two. Our first-round playoff match was against William & Mary College from

Virginia at the Dust Bowl. Our opponents played hard and we had a game-winning goal nullified in regulation time. We played overtime, and lost in a penalty shootout. This was a team we had thumped a couple weeks earlier.

I didn't know it yet, but it was my very last game at the university.

A month after our loss to William & Mary, I wrote a letter that effectively ended my Howard tenure. The letter, to athletics director Leo Miles, was a list of demands for better treatment of the soccer program. I wanted small concessions: A paid assistant to manage the squad and scout the opposition, an ambulance and doctor at home games, and the posting of the soccer team's schedule on the campus display board. I also wanted to be consulted on the purchase of gear. (In 1978, the administration had foolishly bought pointy-toed Pony soccer boots that had tripped up my players.) Finally, I asked for an increased travel allocation so we could leave a day early for distant games. In 1976, our flight had touched down in South Carolina just an hour before the start of our quarter-final match against Clemson. It was no way to prepare for a big match, and we duly lost. I closed my letter to Miles by threatening resignation if my requests weren't heeded.

For seven long weeks, Miles made me sweat. He acknowledged receipt of my letter and promised a meeting. Then . . . *Nada*. Nothing. A sympathetic *Hilltop* staff writer pointed out in an article that "less successful programs" at Howard enjoyed some of the very things I was asking for. He observed that the basketball team (which had never come close to winning an NCAA title) had not one, but two assistant coaches. Still, no word from Miles.

The annual athletic banquet was coming up; my players, led by Jamaican Bancroft Gordon, had rallied to support me. They knew what I was going through. They'd seen me folding uniforms in the locker room late at night because the equipment manager refused to extend us the same courtesy that was given to the American football players. The players called a press conference with the *Washington Post* and the *Examiner* to air their grievances, and sent off a letter outlining the team's needs to Vice-president of Student Affairs Carl Anderson. He didn't take them seriously. Finally, Bancroft and the boys decided to boycott the banquet.

Some of the other teams agreed to boycott too, but as the date of the dinner approached, they pulled out, allegedly under pressure from the Howard administration to shut-up or risk losing their scholarships. On the night of the celebration, my boys littered the chairs at the head table with flyers listing their complaints. These, they wrote, are the reasons we're not here. I remember at least one of their points: At practice, we scrimmage in two sets of nearly identical white jerseys, which makes it hard to tell teammates from opponents. Then, they stood outside handing out flyers to arriving guests. Bancroft says Leo Miles approached him with tears in his eyes and made an impassioned plea to call off the protest. In an act of unabashed deceit, the athletic director also suggested that there were things about me that my team didn't know.

I spoke at the banquet that night. I said that the treatment of teams wasn't fair across the board. Not long after, I got a letter saying that my contract wouldn't be renewed.

Miles fought dirty. After I'd been dismissed, he maligned me in the university press, saying that I had "forged" transcripts for players and "manipulated" them to fight my battles. They were low blows, and quite untrue. The truth was that Miles was bitter about the team suspensions and perhaps a bit jealous of our success. His pet American football team had floundered while we prospered. As for "manipulating" players, my team was faithful to me because I fought for their scholarships and got them fed. I had cared for many of them as if they were my blood.

Twice in my life I'd given management ultimatums. The first time was with the Darts when I told manager Norman Sutherland that I'd leave if he didn't keep paying my salary as a player-coach after he'd stripped me of my coaching duties. That standoff hadn't ended well either. The lesson I walked away from Howard with is that you should never threaten management, whether you have a winnable case or not. From then on, whenever I left a job, I sent a gracious letter, thanking my employer for the opportunity and wishing the organization all future success.

"Something happened one day (in early 1980): it was probably the gear (uniform) thing. Lincoln was giving the pre-match prayer and he started crying. He got choked up. We started realizing there was a campaign against him. We got the idea that they were trying to squeeze him out because he had been speaking out against the treatment of the team."

Bancroft Gordon, Howard University soccer player

"He made a stand. From an economic standpoint, it might not have been the most prudent thing to do. If he feels strongly, he will let the chips fall where they may. I have admiration for him, but I not going to do that."

Victor Gamaldo, lifelong friend and teammate

"The type of things Lincoln was asking for weren't excessive. Basically, he was asking for parity with the football program. But people came to the university because of the American football program. Let's be realistic: Only a small number of people were coming because of the soccer program."

Ernest Skinner, Howard soccer team manager

In my ten years at Howard, we had won 116 and lost just nineteen. We had hoisted two championship trophies (one of which was taken away), and been to the semi-finals three times. We had also been barred from postseason play for a total of four seasons for eligibility infractions. From 1972 to 1980, I had earned the fantastic sum of $32,000 a year, which was good money at a time when gas was just twenty-eight cents a gallon. Playing for the Baltimore Bays, my annual salary had been $7,000. I was probably the first full-time college soccer coach in the United States. Even the hyper-successful Harry Keough of St Louis University had worked for the U.S. Postal Service while coaching his team.

On my way out the door, I told the university press: "Miles treated me shabbily. A coach is a dog down here. It is not fair and I promised myself that I would not go on under this . . . not another year. My plans are personal right now. I don't wish to really go into that, but I could tell you one thing: Anything is much better than staying here under these conditions."

I would soon find out—that was debatable.

14—I'LL TAKE THE JOB

Maryland, USA
1980

I had told the Howard *Hilltop* that anything would be better than staying on as coach under such trying conditions. The statement now seemed quite untrue. Linda and I were scrounging to meet our bills, and the depressing lack of money was making me irritable. I refereed to make ends meet—from youth to junior high and amateur—and ran a few clinics. In summer, I had the Lincoln Phillips Soccer School, but it could hardly meet a year's worth of bills.

I was learning anew that family is the most important thing. Sheldon, my eldest was in high school; Derek, our youngest, was just five. (In the late 70s, Derek had been the unofficial mascot of the Howard soccer team. Whenever I had to keep him, I packed his lunchkit and carried him off to the university where he was petted and doted on.) Perhaps, as Linda and I struggled to keep body and soul together, the boys noticed for the first time that we were not superheroes, but fallible human beings.

And then my father died. I got the call in my bedroom late at night and drifted into the living room, where it seemed that I cried for hours. His friends—and he had a lot of them since he was always liming—sent him off real nice in a solemn funeral on Ash Wednesday in St James. The day after Carnival ended was an appropriate time to lay to rest a man who had so enjoyed playing his bass during the festival.

My Dad had his flaws. He had three families, so the time he spent with his kids was limited. Yet he did his best to give me the things I needed, and encouraged me in sports and school. I respected, feared, and loved him. He protected us, and always took the last cent out of his pocket if we needed it. I had wanted to be like him in many ways. And in some ways, not.

My relationship role model was my neighbour in St James, Clifford Francis Lau. As far as I knew, he was a monogamous man. When I saw him kissing his wife and apparently enjoying himself, I gaped. He blushed. Since then, I had wanted to be a protector—a good husband who protects his family with his life.

At home, to avoid snapping at each other, Linda and I were channeling our energy into renovations. It's a family joke that I am not a handy man. There was ample proof of this in the early 80s. When we began the basement renovation, I cut the drywall with an electric saw, coating myself and the entire house in a shroud of gypsum dust. Alarmed by my ghostly appearance, a friend who stopped by asked to see what on earth I was doing. I was stunned when he pulled out a box cutter, scored the drywall on one side, and snapped it clean in half without producing a speck of dust! Linda also made work easier when she read a book and realized there was no need to balance drywall on her head while attaching it to the ceiling; a simple wooden T-frame did the job just as well, and its neck didn't ache from the strain.

Gaithersburg High School in Maryland had one of the worst soccer teams in the country. In three years, they'd lost thirty-six games. How many had they won? A big fat zero. Soccer Mom Myra Nelson was fed up. Both her sons played for Gaithersburg. (Mike, in particular, was so enthusiastic about the sport, he'd have slept in his boots and uniform.) The Nelsons were good players who had attended several camps where I'd guest-coached, but most of their teammates were . . . *skillfully challenged.*

When the Gaithersburg coach resigned in 1982, Myra learnt that I was no longer at Howard. "You think he might be interested?" she asked her son, Mike. He said she should ask me. Before Myra could finish making her pitch, I was out the door. At home, renovating the house to keep my sanity, I'd been like a soldier looking for war.

"Do you know this soccer team hasn't won a game in three years?" asked Gaithersburg's athletic director after I had signed the contract. In front of her stood the very successful coach of an NCAA championship-winning team, celebrated in the Washington DC metro area. I said I knew, but honestly, I didn't. I just really needed the work.

The next morning at practice, I remarked to myself: "Lincoln, what mess you getting into?" Gaithersburg, a rural area with lots of open farmland, wasn't exactly teeming with soccer talent, but it had to compete against schools from Rockville and Bethesda where good young players were coming through the system. There were three solid players on the Gaithersburg team, including Myra Nelson's two sons. Most of the seniors had never won a game in high school. What could I do?

First of all, I made practice fun. Out in the boonies, with an all-white team, in an area where American football was the only "real" sport, I played Bob Marley. "Guys, you've got to get moving," I urged, as I pumped up the music. (There weren't too many Marley fans out in Gaithersburg.) Secondly, I ran them hard. One morning, they finished what they thought was the final rep of whole-field sprints. As they doubled-over to recover, I said: "Soccer is the biggest liar in the world. Don't take my word for granted. Six more." A senior named Paul Wenninger raised his head and said, "Goddammit, I'm tired of losing." He took off running, and the rest of the team pursued him like hounds.

Finally, I looked for strengths. A player might do eight things terribly and one thing well; I concentrated on the positive. I instructed one tough little player with zero ball control on how to mark an opponent tightly. "Like a leech," I said. "You know what a leech is?" He certainly did, and he took my instruction literally. The opponent, ten times the player my guy was, got so frustrated by the warm breath on the back of his neck that he became totally ineffective. Of course, I christened my guy "Leech."

I had always given nicknames that stuck. At Gaithersburg, some were dispensed because the boys' actual names were too hard to remember, or just better when shortened. Mark Rasavage was big and actually quite a good stopper. Sometimes, however, I'd move him up front to create chaos. "Where's my bull!" I'd yell. "I want my bull in the china shop! Where's my Savage? Put him up top to do some damage." He blundered around knocking down players like bowling pins. From then on, he was "Savage."

Paul Wenninger was a name I could never get right. Hearing the boys snicker after I'd tripped over it for the umpteenth time, I called out: "Wineberg! Steinberg! What's your name, boy? Spell it." The players found it hilarious. "Wineberg! Steinberg!" became a standing joke. My retort was: "Wait until you cross 50."

My friend Keith Collis in Baltimore, I called "Tanglefoot," after a character from the comics. Collis was always tripping himself up. He is the only man I've ever known to cut through a tree that fell *up* rather than down. His wife called me to see it, suspended by vines from surrounding trees. The vines must have pulled taut when Tangle hacked through the trunk. If you told him he'd parked with his back wheel on the curb, he'd jump back into the car and spend some time parking again, ending with *both* wheels on the pavement. When he heard his new nickname, he approached me: "Who it is call me Tangle?" I claimed to have no idea, and blamed it on our friend, Gerry Brown. Tangled believed it too.

Coaching at Howard in the 70s, an African-American student tried out for the team. He couldn't play at all, but wanted to be around us so badly that he asked to be made manager. When the team stopped to eat, the kid would make the rounds, asking if players had finished eating. All leftovers went straight down his throat. "Jesus Christ, you finish all the food?" I joked. "You's Jaws!" In his final year at university, he trained hard and I put him on the roster. We were winning handily one game, so I put him on. The whole bench, and the fans, went crazy. "Jaaaaws!" When we earned a penalty, I let Jaws take it. Unfortunately, he missed.

Many years earlier while playing for the Trinidad and Tobago national team, I had seen a young player from South Trinidad getting dressed in an unconventional way. He had put on his shirt, tie, and blazer, but still hadn't donned his pants. "Look at that," I said. "You doh find he looking like Fred Flintstone?" Thirty years later, he told me that many people swore that Fred was his actual name.

"He gave nicknames to players on the team and generated a kind of *esprit de corps* that was remarkable. You take a bunch of guys who were considered losers and you make them into a team. He made people believe you could do anything."
Mike Nelson, Gaithersburg High School

"Anytime he used your nickname, that was like an injection of adrenaline."
Kenneth "Kendo" Ilodigwe, Howard University

"Somebody pass a ball to me and before it drop, I hit it with my left. Lincoln say, 'Oh God, Spirit!' That's how I got my name. It was from like forty yards out. Even when people go home and talk to my father, they don't know Trevor Mitchell, but they know Spirit."

Trevor "Spirit" Mitchell, Howard University

Spirit's goal was a bit more dramatic than he describes. Howard was playing a tough game against the University of Maryland when he pulled a ball down from a height with his left foot, and hit a volley that crashed off the crossbar and bounced over the goal line. I shouted: "Oh God, Spirit!" because he must have had some supernatural assistance. He couldn't do it again, even in a thousand tries.

In my first year at Gaithersburg, I had told the players that we were the Spoilers. That meant we'd make it a bad day for our opponents by winning every 50/50 tackle and every loose ball. What we lacked in skill and technique, we'd make up for in hustle and desire. "Bad play or mistakes, I'll understand," I said. "But lack of effort, I will never accept."

Early in the season, we beat the state champions 2-1 on penalties. They had trounced the team 10-0 the year before I arrived. The athletic director called me early the next day to say something terrible had happened and she was on the verge of suspending the entire soccer team. Come right away, she said, to see your players' handiwork.

In the euphoria of newfound success, several of the players got carried away. With a few beers swirling in their brains, they broke into an equipment closet, scuttled off with some bags of powdered limestone (used for marking playing fields) and wrote, in huge white letters on the American football field: "G'BURG SOCCER #1" The football coach was livid. "It was stupid," I told the athletic director. "But you can't suspend them for that." The punishment was too extreme. I made the players apologize and erase their graffiti. It was a teachable moment. "People always get in trouble when they're too happy, or too sad," I told them. "You have to manage those periods cautiously, because those are the times when you're apt to do something you'll regret."

We ended the season having won eight games—a record for Gaithersburg—and were only eliminated from the playoffs by a coin toss. A couple players made All-State, and I was voted High School Coach of the Year for Montgomery County, Maryland.

In the second season, the team was still limited in many ways, and I had to swallow my pride. I was a winning college coach who had made history for a historically-black university! Yet, strategizing to make players believe they were better than they actually were was a great experience. It helped me to get the most out of my players in future, when the stakes were higher.

Unfortunately, we lost a few of our better players, and ever more desperate measures were required. Completely outmatched against the state champions who we'd beaten the year before, I threw everyone up front in the hope of scoring a few quick goals and then retreating to eleven men in goal. The guys missed a few early, and the opposition turned around and demolished us. We ate nine. After the match, my players apologized. "Apologize for what?" I asked, in genuine bemusement. "We went out, we had a plan to beat a superior team, and it was unfortunate we didn't get the goals." Poor fellas; they were so accustomed to being abused after losses by roaring coaches.

Yet we did well enough in the first two-thirds of the season that the county newspaper, the *Montgomery Journal*, published a picture of the team on its front page. The caption read: "Gaithersburg playoff-bound." It turned out to be the jinx I feared it would. We didn't win a game after that.

Against Montgomery Blair High School, we were scored upon three times in the first half and four times in the second. Desperately, I sent our goalkeeper to stand on the half-line and told him to boot the ball up to the front. We scored one, we scored two, we scored three. They took a long shot and scored one on us. After the game, a spectator came over and said: "Coach, that was one of the most exciting games I have ever seen." Those were just some crazy things I was able to do in a fun two years.

It was hard to find an athlete at Town and Country Day School in Maryland. The little kids sat all day, listening to rhymes instead of skipping and hopping like jumping beans. The older ones were getting fat. Academics ruled the day.

I was recruited as the school's Director of Physical Education and Athletics by a board member who knew me from my soccer school.

It was the early 1980s and I was in no financial position to refuse. If there was any lingering doubt about the job, it dissipated as soon as I walked into the gym. It was dark, but up on the wall was painted a giant tiger. "Ow!" I remarked. "That's it." The school's teams, such as they were, were the Town and Country Tigers.

Since the kids didn't really want to sweat and the parents thought Physical Education (P.E.) was a distraction from academics, I decided to host a symposium on the importance of P.E. Despite everyone's skepticism, the gym filled with parents and students. My first guest lecturer, an orthopedic surgeon, talked about the benefits of exercise from a medical standpoint, and the head of Howard University's physical education department lectured on incorporating exercises into sport. We told them that the hormone responsible for physical and mental growth, Brain-Derived Neurotrophic Factor (BDNF), is stimulated by movement. It all tied together under the Latin phrase: *Mens sana in corpore sano*—A sound mind in a healthy body. Your kid's brain will improve if her body does!

Phys Ed classes began, and I brought in specialists to coach track and basketball. We pushed basketball games from 1 to 7 pm, and the stands filled up. Team spirit and school pride became concepts that folks could identify with. In P.E. class, I encouraged a pretty South Asian girl who shuffled around with her head down, to shoot some baskets. She couldn't get near the hoop, but I made her keep trying. One day in the gym, I heard jubilant screams. She had scored a basket at last. "What have you been doing with this girl?" asked her teacher. "She's been answering questions in class."

I began to get my way in most that I asked for.

When I suggested to the principal that we paint the drab green gym in a new colour, he told me to get a price. Peppy the painter, a friend of mine, quoted $10,000. I told the principal he could give me $5,000 for the job, if he bought the paint himself. Go right ahead, he said. Linda loves decorating, so she was up for the job and chose a nice white paint.

I know nothing about painting. (As I knew nothing about drywall.) After covering this enormous gym with a single coat, you could still see the green. My wife, her arm already aching from hours atop a scaffold with a roller in hand, now had to help me put on a second coat. If you saw that place when we finished: it looked like someone had switched on the lights.

The administration got a parent to come in to sand and lacquer the wooden floor until it shone like a mirror. And Pepsi was giving away scoreboards, so I went to them and asked for one, admitting that I couldn't sell very much soda. The marketing guy agreed to give me a damaged board if I could send a truck to collect it. The only defacement was a little dent. A parent put up the board and I called the principal. "Come down to the gym," I urged. "Somebody's injured." He raced down there, and stared bug-eyed at our handiwork.

In 1990, Virginia Commonwealth University (VCU) was crying out to be known for something other than art, music, and physiotherapy. Sports were a tough sell. The school didn't have any sporting fields of its own; just a gymnasium. That didn't stop Dr. Eugene Trani, the university's incoming president, from deciding that he wanted a first-class athletics program. He directed his staff to hire full-time coaches for tennis and soccer.

To prepare for the VCU job interview, I wrote out a list of questions that Linda used to grill me. "Too long-winded," she'd say. "Cut that response in half." I also called coaching acquaintance Dave Amsler. Dave was one of the top Under-12 coaches in the country and his club was based in Richmond, close to VCU. He prepped me by telling me about VCU's level of play and the soccer team's culture. He also warned me about two rough-and-tumble brothers from Texas who were wreaking havoc.

I aced the interview and was hired. I was about to move 130 miles from my home in Columbia, Maryland to an apartment in Richmond to deal with a team that had more than a few bad eggs. Fortunately, I'd have the help of Jon Stueckenschneider.

Stueck had been the assistant under the former coach, who had quit after a poor run. With great insight into the nature of the team, he had warned the departed coach not to announce his resignation while he was still trying to lead, but the coach hadn't listened. Sure enough, the effect of the coach saying he was going before he actually left was that the inmates were running the asylum.

Fighting was the biggest problem. Some of the players had reputations on campus for enjoying a good brawl. And sure enough, the battles followed them. Standing in line at a fraternity party one night, the soccer players were provoked by a big, baseball-playing Virginia redneck. "I better not see any soccer players inside," warned the baseball player. "You caused trouble for us last time." Somebody chirped back and the redneck took a swing. For his recklessness, he was properly pummeled.

Stueck and I got the guy's name and went to the baseball coach, who I had a good relationship with. "He's not a main guy," said the coach. "He's a fringe guy. And I heard he got it pretty good, so that's the end of that." I called in the players who were involved and suspended them without prejudice. Like pulling a tooth—POP!— it was done. They knew from then on that I wasn't going to deviate and justice would be swift and fair. I expected good conduct and a commitment to training and academics.

My African-American captain Eric Dade could flat-out fight. He was ably supported by a few unruly players who were quick to get physical when they knew he was nearby. When I got news of yet another team dust-up, I called Eric to my office. He protested that he hadn't fought, and had actually pulled players out of the battle before retreating. I told him he should have known better than to go there in the first place because there was bad blood with the fraternity that hosted the party. I docked some of his scholarship money and took away his captaincy.

Those players so believed in Eric, or "E" as they called him, that six of them came to protest. "Regardless of what you do," said an assistant captain. "E is still our captain." I said that was fine. I brought in a priest to speak to the team (a few of the players were regular churchgoers), and a lawyer who explained the definition of assault. "A simple poke," he said, jabbing at my shoulder with his index finger, "can constitute assault." He told them they needed to walk away. Soon enough, the fighting stopped.

It was a happy day when I reinstated Eric Dade as captain.

VCU had traveled ten uncomfortable hours to Alabama to play the University of Alabama at Birmingham. (If I thought the Howard University administration had shortchanged its soccer team, I was wrong. When VCU traveled to Tampa, Florida, we had to drive twelve hours in a minivan. Englishman Wayne Pratt lay atop the equipment bags in the trunk to avoid being crushed between teammates on the back seat.) The Texan brothers I'd been warned about were both on the trip. The quiet one started in goal; the more volatile was on the bench.

We were up 1-0 in the second half and Alabama was threatening to score when Mr. Texas kicked over our water cooler and swaggered around in a huff. After the match, he tore off his shirt. His face contorted by fury, he yelled: "My #&%!*&@ relative came two hours from Memphis to see me play, and I didn't even see the field!"

Through clenched teeth, I managed: "Stueck, if you don't get this guy out of my face, I'll kill him." Wonderful assistant that he was, Stueck kept us separated for the journey home. I decided not to deal with Mr. Texas that day. On Monday, he was suspended. The whole team heard the gavel's clap as I handed down the sentence. Players understood. Team culture didn't change overnight, but it did change. Although suspended, Mr. Texas showed up for practice. He was suddenly helpful, following instructions and moving equipment without being asked. I put him back on the team.

I still repeat this little piece of advice today: People always get in trouble when they're emotional. Wait until you're calmer to act.

Kwaku Adu-Gyamfi is one of my life's rewards as a coach. The son of a Ghanaian diplomat, Kwaku was playing high school soccer in Northern Virginia when I first saw him. His coach had asked me to come see some players, who were quite ordinary, but among them was a fast, skilful young man. "Who's that?" I asked. "Oh, that's Kwaku," said the coach. He implied that he wasn't worth pursuing because his work ethic wasn't up to scratch. The comment made me feisty, even though it turned out to be true.

Kwaku was lackadaisical, academically and on the field. The guy had a dismal SAT test score that wasn't near enough to get into VCU. But I was intrigued, and Linda was constantly in my skin[38] to give him a chance. With the help of Scotsman John Kerr, who had played with me for the Washington Darts, I got him some SAT tutoring. Kwaku re-sat the test and called when he got his result. If you hear noise on the phone! He was coming to VCU.

At high school, the boy had played on raw talent, but was nowhere near where he needed to be to excel in college. He was talented, selfish, and spoilt. He wasn't prepared for two-a-day training sessions, or

---

[38] Nagging.

the size and strength of teammates and opponents. A couple times a season, I assessed fitness by having players run the Cooper test-two miles in under twelve minutes. Kwaku said it gave him nightmares, and he always came last, if he finished at all.

He also wouldn't follow instructions. He was a good dribbler but he held onto the ball too long, so I instructed the players to kick him every time he touched it. WHACK! WHACK! WHACK! "Play on!" After one practice session, I went to the players and said: "Guys, I have two balls. One is for all of you; the other is for Kwaku. He doesn't like to share." He later told me that he thought at the time: "Wow, not only does this man hate me, but he's trying to get everyone else to hate me, too."

I didn't know it then, but I'd been so tough on Kwaku that he was close to quitting. He was more sensitive to criticism than I'd assumed, and I had risked breaking him. His friends, however, urged him to stick it out. He stayed on campus between his first and second years, to run and lift weights with his teammates, and rocketed from scoring five or six goals a season to scoring fifteen.

In his senior year, after I had left VCU, he scored about forty, which was a record for some time. He earned his undergraduate degree and later went back to school to get his Master's. He played professionally in the North American A-League, predecessor to today's MLS. At the Richmond Strikers youth club, he likes to consider himself an empathetic coach who invests more time in dealing with kids' problems than most others. I guess you could say I'm glad I didn't give up on Kwaku. And that he didn't give up on me.

My first year at VCU, we didn't have very good results. We lost more than we won, but we drew a lot. We were just missing some pieces. People knew that discipline had improved. Caught on campus with his pants halfway down his butt and shoelaces untied, one of my guys claimed he didn't have a belt. I took off my own shoelaces. "Put them around your waist," I said, "and when you get home, bring back my shoelace. And you see that earring in your ears, take it out. When you go out with your girls and they like to nibble your ears, put it in." It got to the stage that when a new guy arrived to see me in my office, the veterans would advise: "Ay, take off your hat." On the road, we stopped at restaurants where servers would comment on my "fine bunch of guys." We only won three games for the season, yet Dr. Trani, the university president, would pass by and comment: "Lincoln, you doing well."

Linda and I had a nice apartment and enough time for evening walks. Life was less hectic than it had been in Maryland, where I'd scrambled from one coaching gig to the next. I was able to do a few clinics for inner-city kids through the YMCA. VCU was still a challenge to recruit to because of the lack of sporting facilities and its slender sporting reputation, but I picked up a couple hot players in Trinidad, including T&T national player Anthony Sherwood. When he agreed to cut his hair, it was the signal that the team was on the rise.

Before the start of VCU's 1994 season, I went to a coaches' lecture. The coach of the Denmark team that had won the 1992 UEFA European Cup told us that he knew his team wasn't as good as the others (they'd only qualified for the tournament because war-torn Yugoslavia had pulled out), so he had been forced to get his players extra-fit. He was talking about my team! The strategy was to win the ball in the attacking third of the field in the first twenty minutes, score, and drop back. In the second half, repeat.

Our season didn't start until September, but I started to run my players hard in January. They didn't like it, and a small delegation approached for an explanation. "Guys," I said, "I don't want to wait until just before the season starts to work on the fitness required for our new strategy." They grumbled.

At a tournament in April, we lost in the final after winning about six in a row. We were tearing teams up. "Coach, this thing working," said the guys, and all agreed to stay for the summer and shave their heads as a sign of commitment.

The rumour was that Anthony Sherwood didn't want to shave his head. He was a good player, on the brink of making the Trinidad and Tobago team, but he was adamant that the hair should stay. (What is it with these young men and their tenacious attachments to their locks?) He returned to Trinidad for the summer.

Several months later, just before the preseason, players were hanging out outside my office when I heard yelling and laughter. Pumped up by our run of success (before this, we'd struggled to win two in a row) the freshly shorn Sherwood announced: "It going to be different this year."

Pancho Wright put me out of the locker room. We'd started the 1994 season on a hot streak-four wins, no losses—and all of a sudden the team didn't need me anymore. "Coach, do you mind leaving the dressing room?" asked Wright—a shifty little mover and one of my co-captains. I was damn vex! The routine was: pep talk, prayer (my mother's 121st Psalm of course: "The Lord shall preserve thee from all evil"), run out onto the field. It never varied. *I* was the motivator: Let no dog bark when I open my mouth!

After a while, they called me back in. The mood was different. Somber. Out they walked in single file without saying a word. If you see football! Our opponent was the University of South Florida. They had regularly handed us five. We put three goals on them that day without reply, but I was still a bit peeved about the disrespect. After the match, I asked one of the players the burning question: "What was that all about?"

"Pancho said we have to take responsibility," he answered. "We shouldn't have to depend on the coach to fire us up." It was a most satisfactory response.

During the preseason, Pancho's Dad had also rallied the team. He invited us to his home and entertained us by the pool. Like me, he was a Christian. "You guys are a good team," he said. "I don't know how you're losing to teams that are lesser than you. You must be like a broom—of one accord." He explained that the strands of a broom could be individually broken, but an entire broom, working as one, could not. "You guys must say the 91st Psalm," he urged. I put the two together and typed it up: "One accord, 91." That was our mantra for VCU's 1994 season, just as Howard's 1974 slogan had been "Truth."

In 1994, we won fifteen matches and lost just three, a remarkable turnaround from figures that were exactly the opposite in my first year. We were only pipped from the playoffs by The College of William & Mary, who had the same number of points but had beaten us 1-0 in our only matchup. We were ranked top twenty in the country and I was voted NCAA Coach of the Year for the South.

Our success in '94 made recruiting easier. I found two outstanding Russian national team players and a Canadian goalkeeper who also played for his national team. They had committed to VCU in principle, but I needed three scholarships to seal the deal. The administration immediately said no, despite having promised additional scholarships if the team did well. I went to plead my case before athletics director Dr. Richard Sander. He was agitated, and adamant. "You're a good coach," he said, warming up quickly in his swanky office. "But if you don't like it, you can take your wares somewhere else."

Ahhh, boy—decision time. I *didn't* like it, but I didn't really want to take my wares elsewhere either. Elsewhere was uncertain. Elsewhere could be a broke and hungry place. On the other hand, my team was on the rise and there was no way I was going to stop three-quarter-way up the mountain. I started meeting with Pancho Wright's father every Monday night in the parking lot of a Hardee's restaurant. We prayed together about the decision.

There were other factors to consider. My youngest son Derek and I were living in a cramped one-bedroom apartment, and Linda had gone back home to Maryland to be with our other sons. Derek was having a hard time at his Richmond high school, where a teacher was picking on him. He moved back home to Columbia.

Then, after two weeks, Dr. Sander called me in for a second meeting. University president Dr. Trani had ordered that I be given a $10,000 raise if I stayed. Sander relayed the news to me. "It's hard times out there," he said. "It won't be easy to find another job." I had already made up my mind. I was going back home to Maryland. For the second time, I was leaving a college coaching job over a difference of opinion with administration.

I learnt some really good lessons at VCU. The first was that I couldn't do without my wife. We had never been apart except for a brief period when I'd first arrived in the United States on professional contract. I missed her love, counsel and companionship. One night I awoke hungry and tried to make a bake.[39] It looked like a Frisbee and tasted like cardboard. The second lesson was that I needed to trust my players by giving them responsibility.

I had sort-of-accepted this in my first year at VCU when I was working on turning a band of battling brothers into a winning soccer team. A sports psychologist intern had spent a week with the team

---

[39]   A roasted Caribbean bread.

and concluded that I was, simultaneously, a good coach *and* the team's biggest problem. "Me?" I asked, befuddled. "Yup," he answered. "If you can get these players to want the game half as much as you want it, the team will start doing well. You gotta give the game back to the team." Linda agreed that I gave my players too hard a time.

So, I pulled back. I let them run the team study hall, held in the library every weekday. The most responsible players administered penalties for late-coming and ensured that guys actually hit the books. I even allowed them to take over some practices. But when the team held my farewell party, they told me: "Coach, just in case you didn't know: we knew you were up in the VCU admin building, peeping at us while we trained."

"He was tough, but he was a father figure. I trusted him. When he was leaving I literally went to his office and cried in front of him. Even though he gave me hell my freshman year, I thought, 'I would do anything for this man.'"

Kwaku Adu-Gyamfi—Virginia Commonwealth University

"I see him as a great, great soccer coach, but what was more amazing about Lincoln was his cunning ability to make us feel individually that nobody could beat us."

Mori Diane—Howard University

"He had that professional approach, having played with high-profile players. But at the time, as a player, I didn't care for his approach."

Sunny Izevbigie—Howard University

"Lincoln never taught me anything about trapping or heading, but he brought discipline and structure. And you don't know how much you could do until you fit enough to do it."

Winston Yallery-Arthur—Howard University

"He presented things in a unique way; such a flair for breaking things down in simple terms. People would clear their schedules months in advance when they knew Lincoln was coming (to host a goalkeeping clinic for kids). He never prioritized anyone, whether it was Tony Meola, or a new kid coming in."

Rudy Rudawsky—physical therapist for US national team

"We remember him the most as a mentor. He's what you call a mentor *par excellence*. He knows how to talk to you and be compassionate. He's been there; he knows how to empathize. As a coach, Lincoln was also good. But I wouldn't say he's the best coach I've had."

David Nakhid—Professional soccer player, T&T national team

"There isn't a day goes by when something happens on the soccer field while coaching and I don't think of something he taught me."

Wayne Pratt—Virginia Commonwealth University, pro-soccer player, soccer coach

"There is only one person that he called 'Coach' and he still calls 'Coach' to this day, and that is Lincoln."

Myra Nelson, mother of Mike Nelson—Gaithersburg High School and all-conference captain at Haverford College

"We did a goalkeeping course in T&T and I was a bit ahead of myself in doing one of my sessions. I had gone on to the next level and advanced more quickly than I should have. Lincoln told me, 'Just follow the program. Don't try to be a bit clever.' He admonished me. It just shows he wanted things to be done right."

Dick Howard, North American Soccer League goalkeeper

"Of course he instilled confidence. When a man that sits at the foot of God in soccer tells you that you can do it, that you're the best, you believe him."

Tom Krebs, father of Clara Krebs—University of Virginia goalkeeper

15—LINCOLN PHILLIPS SOCCER SCHOOL

Virginia, USA
1971

This was rural Virginia. As you walked along the path to the football fields, you had to keep an eye out: There was always a chance of meeting a snake. And after camp ended for the day, the kids had to be checked for ticks.

Howard had just won the 1971 national championship, and the boost in soccer's visibility in the DC Metro Area had earned me an invitation to coach the sport at a big American football camp in Virginia run by ex-Washington Redskins player John Wilbur. The couple days of soccer coaching proved so popular, Wilbur split the camp—one week American football, one week actual football.

I enjoyed watching Redskins wide receiver Charlie Taylor enthusiastically try soccer for the first time. (Receivers are the speedy guys who run "routes" downfield, waiting for the quarterback to sling the ball into their hands.) Charlie retired from football as the NFL's all-time leading receiver in 1977; he was inducted into the Pro Football Hall of Fame in 1984. After fifteen minutes on the soccer pitch, he gasped: "Damn, man, this game is hard."

After the second year at the Camp of Champions, Kelvin "Kello" Joseph, who had stripped the mystery from my courses on the human body when I was pursuing my Physical Education degree, encouraged me to start a soccer camp of my own. "Linco, your name is big enough," he said. "You can do it." I got a $6,000 loan to cover the printing of promotional material and other start-up costs, and went hunting hither and thither for a site. Every one seemed to be booked. Finally, a friend directed me to Garrison Forest, a private girls' school just north of Baltimore, Maryland. It was posh. The sprawling grounds were lush and beautiful. I was sure I wouldn't get it, and then I did.

For the first session of camp in 1975, we had forty players. The second began with just ten. The $6,000 I'd borrowed loomed taller than the venerable trees lining the Garrison fields. Then, a TV news crew came trundling across the field. "What are you guys up to?" asked the reporter. I told him it was the first day of the Lincoln Phillips Soccer School. "Awww, Lincoln Phillips from the Baltimore Bays! That's great," said the reporter. It was mid-week on a slow summer news day, and he was already instructing his cameraman to set up. I got three minutes on the local news that night, and sixty-five kids signed up the next day.

Most of the soccer camps in the area were little more than babysitting playpens at the time. I advertised as a soccer school: **If you aren't serious about soccer, this is not the place to come.** We focused on technique and I drafted good former players as coaches: All-American Ian Bain from Howard University; Victor Gamaldo from the Baltimore Bays, Washington Darts, and the T&T national team; Richard Chinapoo from the New York Cosmos. Kello, my encourager, was a stalwart. He arrived early, stayed late, and remained an annual fixture for almost twenty years, even after a fellow coach put live crabs in his bed as a practical joke.

From Howard, I drafted Jamaicans Bancroft Gordon and Lincoln Peddie, and Trinidadian goalkeeper Trevor Leiba. Milton Miles, trainer to Howard's championship soccer teams of the 1970s, was also a regular camp attendee. When it crossed 100 degrees Fahrenheit, Milton made the call on whether practice should continue. He educated players about the symptoms of heat exhaustion—dizziness and nausea—and tried to ensure that everyone drank enough fluids.

Concerned that a female player might be suffering from heat stroke because she hadn't been drinking enough water on a sweltering summer day, he called an ambulance. When the first responders arrived and took her vital signs, the hospital dispatched an Advanced Life Support team to meet them en route to hospital. She recovered nicely, thanks to Milton's vigilance. He demonstrated the same attention to detail at soccer school as he had at Howard, where players appreciated his meticulous taping jobs.

Each camp session lasted five or six days and I ran several sessions a summer, between seasons at Howard. It was a huge undertaking to feed and house the kids. At orientation, I told the group: "When you leave this school, apart from improving your soccer skills, you'll be able to make your bed." The parents always cheered because many of the kids were excused from chores at home. There was a room inspection each morning, and the kids stood ramrod straight as coaches checked each bed in a dormitory of two hundred. "Pass! Pass! Fail!" On the floor, the shoes were lined off in rows. On the final day, players were expected to strip their beds and put the linens in a pile for the cleaners.

Coaches were also subject to a code of conduct. Richard Chinapoo came running to get me one morning. "Coach, this guy down the road, you hadda fire him," he blurted. "He cussing the girls!" I followed Chinapoo at a trot, only to hear the F-word being booted around by a recently hired coach by the name of Gramaldi. The kids were upset. I took Gramaldi aside. "Ay, we don't do that here," I said. "I'll pay you for the week, but you're going to have to leave." The coaches set the standard and counselors, older players who'd attended camp previously, followed through. The counselors once collared a guy for smoking weed. He was brought to me in disgrace.

Gabor Szemzo, a long-haired Hungarian, liked to run the kids early in the morning. Because I emphasized skills over fitness (I told the kids they could work on fitness when they got home), I had to rein Gabor in. But he was passionate about the game, and passed that passion on. Taken to Trinidad on tour, he fell in love with the local Carib beer, and convinced a bartender at a house party that he should save the few remaining lagers for him. Why? Because Gabor (according to Gabor) was the Russian heavyweight karate champion, visiting for a tournament.

The camp culture quickly gelled around coaches like Tim Lambkin and Philbert Prince—both soccer-playing soldiers from Trinidad who I trusted implicitly. Lambkin was my army "batch." He was #3084, and I was #3085. We had both arrived at the Regiment entrance exam intending to fail and carry on with civilian life. We'd either done a very lousy job of it, or standards had been lowered to ensure that we couldn't escape.

Prince had proven his loyalty back in 1967, when several Regiment players, including myself, had gone to the Pan Am Games to play for

T&T. The players who stayed behind with Regiment wanted to prove that they didn't need the national players to win in the First Division, but soon lost several matches to teams we had grown accustomed to beating easily. When we returned from Pan Am, Prince broke ranks with the jealous clique and admitted he was glad to have us back. He and Lambkin paid their own airfares from Trinidad each summer, but earned enough at camp to make the journey worthwhile.

It might also have been that they came for the lime.[40] When the kids were safely tucked in, the coaches often played cards. Even the world's worst Rummy player, Terrence "English" Whall (Guyana-born, England-raised, and convinced he was Trini) was dealt a hand. English endured constant taunting. He was one of those guys who don't mind being the butt of every joke, and we appreciated his good-natured resilience.

Jamaican restaurateur and football administrator Winston Chung Fah sang (it was one of his many talents) and provided comic relief. During an impromptu cricket match, started largely because Winston had been proclaiming his greatness at the sport, he took his time walking to the wicket, putting on his imaginary gloves, and taking a very precise guard.[41] BADOW! Before he raised his bat, the ball had hit the wicket. Everyone died with laughter, so the match was declared over.

For many of the American kids, camp was a cultural experience; their first extended personal interactions with non-Americans. Suriname's August Wooter, who I had played against in my first international match for T&T, brought his love of calypso to the soccer school; Algerian Abdul El Medhoui represented the French/North African connection; and Bernd Schunk and Volker Piekarski instilled Germanic discipline. A tour to Trinidad made the campers appreciate that not everyone was quite as wealthy as they were, and quite a few gave away their shoes. When we went to Europe, I collated a binder of notes on the cathedrals and museums on our itinerary, and offered to waive the next year's camp fees for the three best written reports.

The female players were a revelation to me. At first, we had very few—maybe five out of a hundred. Among them was Carolyn

---

40 Social gathering where productivity is frowned upon.

41 Where the batsman takes directions from the umpire on the relative position of the wicket behind him.

Cacolice. At the age of eleven, she was already a ball peeyong.[42] She hung around the coaches when we showed off our skills and then snuck away to practice alone for hour upon hour. If she didn't master a trick during that session, she'd certainly have it down for the next year's camp. When next you saw her, she'd juggle the ball with her feet, catch it on the nape of her neck, and go down for a pushup. She once gave me a tremendous headache and cost me quite a bit of money.

I had put out a challenge to all players: Anyone who could curl a ball into the goal from the corner flag would get a $560 scholarship to the next year's camp. You had ten tries to do it. Led by Carolyn, four kids did it in just three days, and I had to shut down the competition. I later found out that she had been competing with a boy one year ahead of her in high school, but I strongly believe she had the advantage; she could do it with either foot. Carolyn came to camp for years until she was old enough to be a counselor. When she was a senior at high school, I called the women's coach at the University of Massachusetts and told him he had to give this girl a schol. Coach Kalekeni Banda had never seen Carolyn play, but he took my word for it and gave her a half-scholarship. She started every game in her four years with the Minutewomen, was voted "All New England," and held the record for most assists in women's college soccer for many years.

I enjoyed coaching women and girls. Years after the Lincoln Phillips Soccer School had wound up, I was appointed women's goalkeeping coach at Loyola University of Maryland. In between, I helped out with a women's recreational team called the Grapes of Wrath. Even though they were skillfully challenged they had great fun competing against such evocatively-named teams as Hot Flashes. While training them on crossovers, they had no qualms about stopping to chat while exchanging the ball. Some of the less serious players would sit on the sidelines talking about children and pedicures. The talk was so nice, they mightn't even want to go on as substitutes! I had just lost my job at Howard, was scrimping to pay the bills, and was very depressed. Their spirits buoyed me.

After five years at Garrison Forest, we moved on. The school only had two fields, and the camp had grown enough that we needed three or four. But wherever we went in Maryland or Northern Virginia, the

---

[42]   Ball-hound.

Lincoln Phillips Soccer School was a big draw. Soccer parents knew the Tiger; I had put the creature, bounding, on the camp logo.

For twenty-three years, camp was a big part of my family's life. In its heyday, we had four hundred kids a week. Linda cooked and handled registration, God bless her, and her sister, Eula, helped with the accounts. My son Sheldon was a counselor who spent a fair amount of time chasing girls. He called it a "weeks-long slumber party with your buddies." All four of my sons were involved; each to a different degree.

Ultraman didn't much care for soccer. He played a decent game (he had his father's genes, after all), but when he'd had enough, he withdrew. Ultra, my third son Gregory, had earned his nickname because he loved the idea of guns. As a boy, he was always pretending to shoot something, making the animated sounds that boys do when engaged in such a fantasy.

At camp, coach Winston Chung Fah was running his players one day when he noticed that Ultra was dawdling. "What happened?" he asked. "I'm tired," responded Gregory. He'd had enough, and wasn't about to push himself anymore. During a game, I might see him plucking grass and tossing it in the air. He admitted early that soccer wasn't his thing, and I had to accept that one of my sons hadn't fallen in love with the sport.

Of our four sons, he seemed the most obedient. In fact, he was politely insubordinate. He agreed with everything I told him, but as soon as he walked out the door, Greg did what Greg wanted. He may have been the least robust, but he forged his body into his machine, joined the Navy, and made it very close to becoming an elite Navy SEAL. Only the vision test kept him out.

It was Greg's car accident that showed Linda and me that we'd done a decent job of raising our boys.

It was the night before Thanksgiving, and cold. Greg's wife called at 3 am. "Don't panic," she said, "but Greg was in an accident. A helicopter took him to hospital." We weren't allowed to see him when we arrived at Maryland Hospital in Baltimore. He'd been outside in the cold for so long that they had to warm him up before doctors could even diagnose his injuries.

Greg, it turned out, had skidded off the road and hit a tree in a rural area. A child in the nearest house had woken her father to say that she heard someone whistling outside. Her father told her to go back to bed, but she insisted: Someone was whistling. When the man went to check, he saw a mangled car, and Greg heading towards the woods in a semi-conscious daze.

My sons were scattered to the wind: Sheldon in law school in Alabama, Sean in Virginia, and Derek in Germany playing soccer. Sean, the nearest, arrived the next day. I told Sheldon that he should concentrate on his exams; we could do without him. He, too, rushed to his brother's side. Derek hopped on a plane and crossed the Atlantic Ocean. I had no idea what day of the week it was.

Greg spent a month in a coma, with collapsed lungs and serious damage to his knees. After a while, his brothers sent Linda and me home. We took turns being at his side, but two of his siblings were always there. When Greg recovered, I thought of that month as the time when I discovered that our sons had listened when we spoke. Like me, they were protectors. And that made me proud as anything.

Sheldon and Sean looked like twins for a while. Just ten months apart, we always joked that Sean was an "Oops." They both loved camp. Being among former professionals was their paradise. They were outstanding for their age: Sheldon, quick and forceful; Sean, slower and skilful. Derek came almost ten years after those two, but by the time he was five, he wanted to be at camp with his brothers. He cried his heart out when his mother took him home at the end of the day. He was still too young to stay overnight.

With so many Caribbean "uncles" around, all my sons were cocooned in West Indian culture, and grew up, to some extent, with a connection to the Caribbean. Derek always longed to go back to the land of his birth and play in national colours. He eventually did, although his stint was short-lived. Sheldon, who has worked in and around soccer administration since the 1994 World Cup in the United States, recently went to Trinidad to take up a position as general secretary of the Trinidad and Tobago Football Federation.

In Maryland and Virginia, all four enjoyed a reflected glory in soccer circles. Sheldon remembers as a little boy, barely big enough to see out of the car window as we drove, hearing people call out:

"Tiger!" They were fans of Howard and the Baltimore Bays. Many of them, I didn't know by name. When I played for the Bays, Sean was a ball boy, and my teammates treated him like he was special. He went on to play professionally and now coaches an NCAA Division III team at Notre Dame of Maryland University in Baltimore.

Camp sessions always yielded a homesick kid. Ten-year-old Danny Liparani had begged his father, owner of the Baltimore Bays, to come to camp. He sobbed through his first night and his parents wanted to come get him right away, but I urged them to leave him just a bit longer. I passed Danny onto Philbert Prince.

Prince somehow lured Danny into becoming curious about what he was drinking. As Danny got close, Prince confided that it was a special Gatorade, used by basketball superstar Michael Jordan. "When Mike drinks this," said Prince, pointing to Jordan on the label, "he gets so strong that he isn't afraid of anything." Looking around warily, Prince offered a swig. Danny's eyes widened as he took the bottle from his lips. "I feel really good," he said. At the talent show at the end of the session, Danny made us laugh until our bellies hurt by gyrating most unabashedly to "Dollar Wine"—that year's hot calypso from Trinidad.

Danny won the Tear-Jerker Award that week—a soccer ball signed by the entire camp staff and presented with the encouraging words: "Your parents are so very proud of you, and your coaches are too. You went through a real difficult time in your life and you won! You won because you were tough." As usual, the award brought the tears down. The following year, the camp photographer captured Danny sitting on a ball, lecturing that session's homesick kid.

Another memorable tragicomedy was a boy who looked like he was on the verge of crying every time you saw him. He was allergic to bee stings, and was stung by a bee on his very first day. The kid walks up to me, looking like he's about to gush. "Mr. Phillips," he says (SNIFF SNIFF), "I can't tell you how much fun I'm having."

This became a long-running joke with my friend, college coach Fred Schmalz, who also coached at my camps. Howard University had a particularly strong team when we went out to play Fred's team at Davis & Elkins College in West Virginia. We had given them four unanswered goals when Fred walked over to our bench and said in a croaky voice: "Mr Phillips . . . I can't tell you how much fun I'm having."

The weekly talent show provided more than enough comedy. As dreadful as the talent could be (for which they were soundly booed) there was usually at least one outstanding performance. At one show, a counselor walked onstage with a duffel bag, his brood of ducklings bobbing along behind to their chosen music. When the counselor opened that bag, a tiny guy emerged, swaying just like a charmed cobra. The place erupted. At another show when the talent was particularly bad, the last group did the Gong Show. Each act was loudly gonged, until a little girl rushed in, begging to be allowed to perform. "I was stuck in traffic," she pleaded. The host relented. When the tinymite started singing, mouths fell open. No one could believe the voice that flowed from that little source.

Over twenty-plus years, LPSS grew to be the premier summer soccer school in the region of Washington DC, Maryland and Virginia. High school coaches brought their teams to us to get them ready for the season. They were exposed to good competition and specialist training. But by the early 1990s, the school was no longer a viable business.

The competition had grown around us. European-run day camps had popped up like mushrooms, making it hard to run a profitable overnight school. Universities were also renting their facilities to their own coaches at discounted prices, who could then turn profits on lower camp fees.

I still get a kick out of being stopped by people who recount their memories of the Lincoln Phillips Soccer School. (I haven't changed much, but they're a lot taller.) The school helped develop some of the best talent in the region. Many of our players, boys and girls, went on to play at college and in the pros. Quite a few have become successful soccer coaches themselves.

My professional soccer career was coming to an end. As calypsonian David Rudder sang of a great West Indian fast bowler, I was learning what it meant to fall short of expectations.

Way Down Under, a warrior falls
Michael Holding falls in the heat of the battle
'Michael shoulda left long time!'

I heard an angry brother shout.
Caribbean Man—that . . .
That that that is the root of our troubles.

As far as I knew, there was no clamour for my retirement, but I could definitely feel the creaks. It was 1974. I had been playing soccer at the national, semi-professional and professional levels almost constantly for eleven years. If you counted high school and college, I'd been hurling myself around for over twenty years. I was 33-years-old.

Victor Gamaldo, who'd played with me at every stage of my career, could see that I was slowing in my last two years with Baltimore. (The team's name had been changed from the Bays to the Comets.) He said I no longer committed with quite the speed and efficiency I once had. In the locker room especially, I felt it.

I used to be a beast at warming up! Stripped to my socks, I slathered my body in Bengay (which you'll know is no joke at heating up the muscles if you've ever mistakenly applied it to your groin) and stretched and jogged on the spot. All this was done before the other players arrived. After my private warm-up, I joined the team for the team warm-up. By the time I took the field, I was drenched in sweat.

In 1974, I could no longer get to that point. On the field, I sometimes felt a little twitch—warning of a lurking strain.

My attention was also divided. Howard consumed much of my time, and in the summers I had a camp to run. Alvin Henderson, who played for Howard and with the Bays, said he could have seen me playing into my forties, but since I was concentrating so much on coaching, he thought I wasn't doing enough to warrant keeping the number one spot. Fortunately, I had a good backup.

Alan Mayer was a 22-year-old fresh out of college. He could stop a ball point-blank, but lacked experience. He'd only picked up the sport as a sophomore in high school, where he played basketball. One season, he thought he'd get into shape for basketball by picking up soccer. The coach put him in net after the starting goalie had conceded five. He loved it and stuck with it.

In the '74 season, I started almost every game for the Comets, but the few times I didn't feel one hundred percent, I told the coach I was injured so Alan could have a sweat. It wasn't *faking*, exactly. It was more like *embellishing*. The last and only time I'd actually feigned injury was back in the early 1960s, playing a match that pitted the best from North Trinidad against the pick of the South. We, the North, were under-strength, particularly in defence. Most of the good Maple players had opted not to play because they were saving themselves for a big match a couple days later.

Near the start of the match, a lampy-pampy[43] defender lost a ball that I'd called for, and the opposing forward buried it. By the third goal, my defence had disintegrated, and I went sour. The fourth was a parody, ricocheting off my arm and rolling in. North was down by four at the half, the crowd was jeering and laughing, and I certainly wasn't relishing the thought of four more. As I approached the coach, I started to limp. "Conrad," I said, clutching my hamstring. "I feeling a little thing . . ." Conrad told me I had to stay in, but started looking around for my backup, Jean Mouttet, who was trying to blend in with the spectators in the stands. "Where Jean?" called Conrad. Luckily for me, a Good Samaritan pointed him out. As Jean passed me, he growled: "You's a real beast. I know you not injured." He swallowed four of his own.

In Baltimore, Alan Mayer played well when given the chance. He went on to have eighteen seasons as a professional and earned six caps for the U.S. national men's team. He later said that it was nice for him to sit for most of the 1974 season and watch and learn from me, on and off the field. As always, I enjoyed the mentor's role.

My final professional match was a North American Soccer League quarter-final against the Boston Minutemen on Astroturf at Alumni Stadium in Boston. There, I met one of the first black men to break into the European leagues, Ade Coker. Coker was a 20-year-old Nigerian striker, on loan to the Boston Minutemen from England's West Ham United. In the first half, he stretched me out with a shot and I went down hard on my left side. At the half, I told the coach I was hurting. Neither team had scored a goal. "Stay on," he said. Five minutes before the end, Coker hit a volley up in the corner. It took everything I had to get to it, and I came down hard again. The ball was right next to me! On the goal line! And I couldn't get up to grab it. It was poked into the net before I could move. Off the field I limped, headed to retirement. We lost that knockout match 1-0. I was given player of the game.

---

[43] Ineffective.

My goalkeeping days were behind me, but my days of coaching United States national team goalkeeper Tony Meola in the 1990s were yet to come. I was hired to coach Meola because I'd qualified as a United States Soccer Federation (USSF) coach in the 1970s.

West Germany's legendary director of coaching Dettmar Cramer had been hired by the Americans to revamp soccer coaching in the United States. I was responsible for soccer at Washington DC's Recreation Department, so they'd given me the job of taking Cramer around to clinics so he could check out the area coaches. The "Football Professor" was only 5' 3", but I quickly realized that my knowledge of the game didn't even reach his ankle.

At half-time of a soccer match between two Virginia teams, the players were expecting him to give the talk. He turned to me: "You go ahead." I'd been coaching for years; half-time talks were second nature. Cramer liked what he heard, and invited me to attend a USSF coaching course. Licensing courses didn't appeal to me at the time. I only went because of him.

I began at the lowest level, the D-license. By 1980, I had worked my way up to the highest level of coaching certification in the United States, the A-license, and started coaching coaches for certification. I was one of the top college coaches in the country, and known nationwide.

Meola was a brash New Jersey boy. He had what young people today would refer to as swag. And he didn't particularly get along with US head coach Bora Milutinovic—in part because he spoke his mind, didn't take any crap, and was likely to pack his bags if you ticked him off. Bora had been hired to prepare the U.S. team for the 1994 World Cup in the United States. The task was an uphill one; the Americans had been spanked in the 1990 World Cup, losing all three matches. Fortunately for Bora though, he had a couple years to make an impact. He wanted to go outside the U.S. to hire assistant coaches, but the USSF insisted that the American coaches were good enough. "Hire them," ordered the federation. So, USSF coach Timo Liekoski got picked as Bora's assistant. He in turn picked me.

Meola and I hit it off. Unlike the other goalkeeping coaches who tried to impress Bora by working their charges until they were battered and bruised from nonstop diving, I ratcheted back the intensity, allowing little breaks where Meola and I could chat about the game.

Meola had the experience of the 1990 World Cup under his belt, and while he wasn't the most technically correct goalkeeper on the U.S. team, he had a knack for coming up with big saves in big matches. Bora respected our synergy. "Mr. Phillip," the Serb would say in his muddled Serbian-Mexican accent, "I don't know what it is with you and Meola. When you not here . . . hmmmmm." He made the universal sign for just so-so. "When you are here—Mama Mia!"

Over the next year, I worked with Meola often, and the other US keepers—Brad Friedel and Kasey Keller—less frequently. The American team had mixed results at the Copa America, the Concacaf Gold Cup, and the inaugural US Cup, but the keepers generally played well. I was almost certain I'd be going to the World Cup finals as a member of the coaching staff. And then, Bora picked a Yugoslav countryman as his goalkeeping coach. The ethnic slaughter of the Yugoslav Wars was on, and Bora told me he had picked his compatriot to get him out of the war. Even if true, it was little comfort.

Meola and I were not done though. He had a great World Cup, and returned to play pro soccer in the U.S. for many years. In 1999, he blew out his knee while practicing for the Kansas City Wizards, and underwent surgical reconstruction of his anterior cruciate ligament. The doctors gave him zero chance of playing again. His rehab was long and painful, much of it done by US men's team physical therapist Rudy Rudawsky.

Three times a week I drove two hours out to Delaware to help Rudy ease Meola back in before he was cleared for training. Rudy picked me because he knew Meola and I got along; he also said that I had a "keen eye for the quality of the movement," which means that I spotted physical limitations and took breaks before problems got too serious. I was especially sensitive about Meola's dodgy knee; at the age of 58, my own knees were going. On the way back to the car after rehab, I betrayed my own incipient limp. (I had both troublesome hinges replaced in 2009.)

In 2000, Meola's first season back after injury, the Kansas City Wizards faced the Chicago Fire in the MLS championship match in Washington, DC. The Fire blazed Meola with ten shots on goal, including three in the final ten minutes. He stopped every one of them, and the Wizards raised the cup. I saw the guy at a hotel after the match, sitting at a big table with all his relatives. He nearly knocked me down with a bear-hug. He always said that I had taught him a natural Caribbean movement and an easy change of direction. I took it as a tremendous compliment when he declared: "You could say he taught me to dance."

"The Cool Cat" camp t-shirt, voted by campers as the most creative design.

One of LPSS's founders— Heino Harbeck.

Kelvin Joseph— Camp meant everything to Coach "Kello".

Philbert Prince—LPSS coach and my Regiment batch mate.

Tim Lambkin— creator of the highly successful end-of-session talent shows.

LPSS coaching staff for the camp's second year: (Front row, L-R) Winston Chung, Terrence "English" Whall, Trevor Leiba, Betty-Jo Scott, Leroy Taylor, Victor Gamaldo. (Back row, L-R) Ian Bain, Fred Schmalz, Milton Miles, Reid, Ty Ferré, Me, Kelvin Joseph.

Campers get a steelpan
lesson on tour to Trinidad.

Karl-Heinz Heddergott—
Germany's director of
coaching, and LPSS coach.

Charlene (L) and Alyssa
Gamaldo—Campers
turned counselors.

U.S. national team player
Desmond Armstrong with his
counselor Whitney Keiller at camp.

The boys and girls of the Lincoln Phillips Soccer School.

Danny Liparani, once a homesick camper himself, counsels a teary-eyed kid.

LPSS staff (L-R)—Coaches Richard Chinapoo and Bernd Schunk, trainer Margaret Shields, chaperone Linda Schultz, boss Lincoln Phillips.

"Professor" Volker Piekarski.

Christian and Manny Lee (R) from the Town and Country Prep School head off to Europe with the camp.

Top-Flight Goalkeeping Academy Super Camp at Cocoa Beach, Florida.

Virginia Commonwealth University players
Eric Dade (R) and Anil Roberts host a clinic
for inner-city youth in Richmond, Virginia.

Jon Stueckenschneider—VCU assistant
coach and Honorary Trini. Easily the best
assistant I've ever worked with.

My four sons, of whom I am very proud.

Sheldon, the eldest—currently
General Secretary of the Trinidad
and Tobago Football Association.

Gregory, my third—who served
with the US Navy; currently a
Brinks security specialist.

Sean, our second—former pro soccer
player, now on the staff of the Notre
Dame women's soccer program.

Sean with the Cleveland Crunch, a
professional indoor soccer team.

Derek, our youngest—in
action for Trinidad and Tobago
against Guatemala.

Derek.

My pride and joy—my six grandchildren.

Eight-year-old Tyler-Max is
leaning toward the Sciences.

Zara, 20, is eyeing a
modeling career.

Five-year-old Joy can already
do twenty pushups!

Marco, 18, writes songs
and plays the piano.

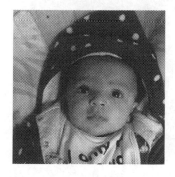

Three-month-old Kenzee—
she is a cutie!

Jah, 13, identified for Maryland's
Olympic Development
Program for soccer.

Standing for the American anthem while serving as goalkeeping coach to the United States team at the U.S. Cup in 1992. Head coach Bora Milutinovic is at left.

Two of my players—United States goalkeepers Brad Friedel (L) and Tony Meola.

The T&T team before the final World
Cup qualifier against Bahrain.

GOOOOOOOL!!! Dennis Lawrence (far right) sends a
tiny nation into fits of ecstasy by scoring the goal that
sent T&T to the 2006 World Cup in Germany.

16—JACK STRIKES BACK

Port-of-Spain, Trinidad
2009

Jack Warner is a practical man. As a politician, his alliances are always temporary, his loyalties fleeting. I started my stint as technical director as a hometown hero, remembered from the gilded age of local football, and it was useful for him to treat me well. For over a year, he paid my salary himself. But I never became one of his boys—that little group of scotch-drinkers who massaged his ego and hopped to his commands. That was where I went wrong.

They came for me with an invoice. It seems a strange article to hang a man with, but in the world of high-politics, it is entirely appropriate. The mob strung me up with a doctored slip of paper.

After the dismissal of Wim Rijsbergen (a victim of his own temper), the T&TFF appointed former national team captain Russell Latapy as national team coach. The attacking midfielder better known as "The Little Magician" had glowing professional and national team credentials. He had played with Portuguese clubs, including Porto, and prospered in the Scottish League with Hibernian. With the T&T team, he had won seventy-nine caps in a twenty year career. He had served as national team assistant coach, but some felt he wasn't head coach material. They said he was indisciplined and got away with rule-breaking because of his brilliance as a footballer. I, however, backed him.

I felt it was time to try a local again. Foreigners with fewer credentials had already been given the job. (Like Rijsbergen.) Latapy had tons of experience at the highest level, and consistently outsmarted people with his cheekiness. Some of that cunning would serve him well as a coach, in coming up with tactics. The senior team was also in transition after the 2006 World Cup, and there was no major tournament in sight. If there was any time to give the man a chance . . .

The T&TFF administration had systematically dismantled my duties in order to get rid of me. By 2009, I was technical director in name alone. I had little work to do, but was still being paid. It irked me to take a salary for work that was not being done, but every project I picked up was snatched from my grasp or attacked.

I had conducted thorough player screenings at the Under-17 and Under-19 levels, even looking for players in areas that had traditionally been ignored—the rural north coast, the communities of majority Indian Central Trinidad, and Point Fortin, which was so far from the "centre" that no one paid it much mind. The teams were headed to the Dallas Cup in Texas to test themselves against top youth teams from the Americas, Africa, and Europe. At the last minute, the administration said the teams weren't ready. They started new screenings, which I was not involved in.

Even my successful coaching certification program was under fire. They said I was giving away the D-licenses (the lowest level of certification) because the exams were open-book. The fact is that you had to know the book to use it properly in the time allotted. And the tests examined the required areas: laws of the game, methods of coaching, tactics, and care and prevention of injuries. I was constantly having to defend my work.

Now, they'd decided to appoint me as goalkeeping coach under Latapy. Here I was, 68-years-old with two brand-new knees, coaching under a man unlikely to succeed. I was later told by a T&TFF board member that Latapy had been hired to fail. I was placed there to fail with him.

Ahhhh, the invoice. It was a big one—TT $250,000 (US $40,000) for footballs, cones, and practice vests for my coaching development program. The equipment had been delivered to the T&TFF office and I'd distributed some of it to teams in the Southern region, but most of it was still stacked in my office, filling every nook and cranny. I found it strange that teams in the other regions hadn't been eager to collect the equipment they had long cried out for.

Soon enough, I got a call from a member of T&TFF staff. "Do you know anything about the equipment? Did you sign for it? Did you order it?" The tone was accusatory, and the interrogation was soon followed by a letter saying that I'd been suspended with pay, pending an investigation into the equipment order. When I told my half-brother Georgie, he started to wheeze. My son Sheldon, a lawyer by training, said he would leave Maryland for Trinidad the very next day. In the meantime, I was called to account.

At the meeting, Jack Warner requested a copy of the equipment invoice. He walked into the interrogation room, waving a faxed copy. I sat there, like a common criminal. "Look at this! Your name is on it!" Indeed it was. Between the first and second lines of the fax was typed: **Lincoln Phillips**. I was ordered to do an inventory. With my wife's help, I counted for hours: 9,000-plus cones, 14,000-plus practice vests. The shortfall in numbers was made up by the total distributed to the South zone. Everything tallied. Yet, I was still on suspension.

Here comes my first-born son. Sheldon demands to see the original invoice. It is headed T&TFF, St Vincent Street, Port-of-Spain, just as the faxed copy was. But my name is not on it. My name is not on it! All that is left is for the Sport Company, a government agency, to admit that they ordered the equipment. They do.

Who wanted me out so badly that they had doctored an invoice to set me up? I know, but I am not telling you. Let's just say that the lust for power and position is very powerful. Jack Warner, whether he knew of the plot or not, had failed to stand up for me. He acted shocked when I told him I was still on suspension, despite having solved the "mystery" of the quarter-million dollar invoice. He said the whole misunderstanding would be dealt with. It was not.

Eventually, I got my termination letter from the Trinidad and Tobago Football Federation. It said: "We are unable to renew your contract." My wife and I were given less than a month to vacate the T&TFF-rented house. A week before the federation's deadline to vacate, Linda had the place spic and span. We gave all our furniture away. I did not fight my dismissal, or make any noise to the press. On May 25, 2009, after six tumultuous years in Trinidad, we were returning to Maryland.

"I don't think Lincoln was unprepared, but he wasn't ready for the politics. He didn't quite realize the organization (T&TFF) was so inefficient. It wasn't an organization; it was one man who everybody did the bidding of. Warner never wanted an efficient organization, which is transparent and accountable. They function better in chaos. That's what Lincoln's programs were—they were efficient and transparent."

Dr. Alvin Henderson—T&TFF technical committee and Howard University player

"I didn't like how he was treated in Trinidad: People got the impression that he was a walkover, a pushover. The Lincoln I knew back in Washington would have fought those battles more than he did in Trinidad. I know he was reaching out to people, but he never got the support."

David Nakhid—T&T assistant coach, also coached by Lincoln

"He is not a political animal. Lincoln cannot survive in that kind of politicized viper-den environment."

Ian Bain—Howard University player

"It was the weakness of a football association that did not have the quality of people to deal with him. Those fellas know so much less than he knows . . . In order to uplift themselves, they sort of downgraded him."

Alvin Corneal—T&T national team teammate

"There has to be a learning curve—and that involved readjusting to an environment he had left thirty years before. He was adjusting to a culture that was not quite as rigid and disciplined as that which he left. He got some unnecessary pressure before he got halfway up that learning curve."

Raymond Tim Kee—T&TFF president, 2012—

"He could have been in the circles of Jack Warner and maybe got some of the things (football development plans) done, but it means that he would have had to compromise himself. Just the mere idea that he didn't, tells you who the man is."

Ken Butcher, former Sport Company CEO

"When Lincoln takes on these jobs, 110% of his time goes into the task at hand. Not too much time is spent on the political side of it: Let me see how to maneuver. By the time he realizes it's important, it's too difficult to manage. When it comes to certain things in soccer, he has tunnel vision."

Victor Gamaldo—lifelong teammate and friend

"Lincoln is arguably one of the best, if not the best, goalkeepers this country has produced. But under his tenure, we never got a goalkeeping coaching program going, and therefore he was open to criticism. I spoke to him about it as technical director. We never got one goalkeeping coaching course, and therefore he was vulnerable to attacks."

Keith Look Loy—T&TFF technical adviser, Howard University player

As technical director, I had certified over 850 coaches and was in the process of implementing a well-defined structure for national youth teams based on a hybrid of the Dutch and Australian academy systems. I had not focused on goalkeeping because it was not yet a priority. There was too much other work to be done. Besides, the football administration executive never suggested that a goalkeeping coaching program was urgently needed.

While I was in Trinidad, three national teams qualified for World Cups—the men's senior team, the Under-17 boys, and the men's Under-20s. Something was being done efficiently, although I can hardly claim that it was all my doing.

I still owe Trinidad a debt. It was there that I learned the game. I remain ready to contribute wherever my skills are needed. But next time, it'll be on my terms.

17—WE BETTER THAN THEM

Alabama, USA
1995

I always told my players that no one could beat them; now, I needed someone whispering the same to me. That person was Tom Krebs. Tom was a hard-nosed lawyer who used an anti-discrimination law referred to as Title IX[44] to ensure that female college athletes got the same funding and opportunities as their male counterparts. His daughter, Clara, was an athletic teenage goalkeeper, but under the pressure of her father's overpowering personality, she had wilted. She needed a coach, and in 1995, one year after I'd left VCU, Tom found me.

Here was this white Alabaman, an ex-marine and former rugby player, calling on me—a black man from the Caribbean—to come down to Alabama, a state made infamous during the Civil Rights movement by the murderous actions of white racists. Tom flew me into Alabama a couple days before Clara had a tournament. My son Sheldon, who was in Alabama working for the World Cup, began slinging balls at Clara from close range, forcing her to get up and down as quickly as she could. She seemed capable, but she was diving over the balls. "I know you're a better goalkeeper than that," I said. "What's the problem?" She began to cry. "It's my Dad," she said. "He puts a lot of pressure on me." There was only one way to comfort her. "Did your Dad play goalkeeper?" I asked. "Forget him. I know more than him."

---

[44] Before Title IX, a college could have twelve men's teams to zero women's. If there were women's sports, they could get away with paying the coaches much less than the men's.

After a few sessions, Clara had what she refers to as the best game of her life. Her body started reacting instantly, seemingly without thought. When Tom Krebs asked what the hell I had told his daughter, I said: "I told her that you don't know what the hell you're talking about." After that, Clara wouldn't allow her father within one hundred yards of her on the field.

I was good for Clara. I called her by her middle name, Tatum. During training breaks, I told her about playing against Pelé and earning the nickname Tiger. She called me El Tigre, and I returned the compliment by naming her La Tigra, saying she had reflexes every bit as good as mine. Her confidence came roaring out. But Tom and Clara were also good for me. I had made a mistake in leaving VCU and I was already feeling the financial pinch. Not only was Tom paying me $1,000-plus per session, but I felt like a coach again. Tom's confidence in me restored my confidence in myself. He also introduced me to a friend, fellow Alabaman Russ Polhemus.

Russ was a speed and agility coach who ran an athlete training facility called the Sport Medicine and Fitness Institute in Birmingham, Alabama, site of the 1963 church bombing that killed four African-American girls as the city struggled with racial integration.

His son, Todd, was a 16-year-old goalkeeper. Pressured by his father just as Clara had been by hers, Todd was paralyzed by overanalysis. His father was intense—the type of Dad who yelled things from the stands until a coach got so fed up that he'd bench the poor boy. And Todd was a Type A personality himself, driven to compete and perform. Not only did I help him with the essentials of the position, but I eased back the intensity. He stopped trying so hard, and everything seemed simpler.

In 1995, Russ Polhemus had lunch with me while I was running a summer camp. I remarked that 1996 was going to be a great year for me. The certainty enveloped me. "I hate to burst your bubble," said Polhemus, "but great things are already happening for you." Tears rolled down my cheeks as it sank in that life was pretty good. I had a loving family, enough work to get by, and I was shaping kids like Todd Polhemus.

Russ sent me off to the airport that day with an envelope. The little card inside said: "Dear Lincoln, I appreciate what you're doing for Todd and me. This is a token of my appreciation." Inside was $4,000. It was just what I needed to get up to date on my mortgage.

Russ later christened one of the fields at his training facility the Lincoln Phillips Field. They play mostly lacrosse there, but I really don't mind. The recognition means a great deal.

I trained La Tigra for months at my soccer camp in Maryland before she went on to play in goal for the top-ten ranked University of Virginia. (She only got the chance to start after two goalkeepers ahead of her were hurt, but she didn't relinquish her position after that.) Clara continued to consult with me about her goalkeeping and life choices for years after our first tearful training session. She was in the pre-medical program at the university when she called to talk about whether she should continue playing soccer. "You had your fling," I said. "You're not going to play professional because there is no professional women's soccer." I reminded her that she had learned good time management in her years of juggling studies and soccer; now she had to devote her extra time to the books. Clara is now a family medicine physician practicing in Hawaii.

My premonition about 1996 being a good year turned out to be spot-on. Masters Press, a niche publisher of sporting titles, helped me get my previously self-published training book "Soccer goalkeeping: The last line of defense, the first line of attack" to market, earning me useful royalties for several years. And Nike gave me a $40,000, four-year sponsorship contract to use its branded equipment at my soccer camps.

Things really change: Two white guys from Alabama had helped me through a difficult time. But those acts of individual generosity didn't change the fact that immigrants are discriminated against. At Howard, we had experienced hostility from whites because of our complexions, and I had also endured the resentment and suspicion of African-Americans who found West Indians haughty. To an extent, it was true: As foreigners, we held our own preconceived notions about black American culture. The spin we'd been given was that black folks didn't cherish education. It was only when we arrived in the U.S. that we learnt the proud history of African-American accomplishment, and found that the denial of education had been systemic.

I have found that prejudice wafts away when the curtains that divide us are briefly drawn. I once attended a coaches' convention in Texas with my fellow coach and friend Fred Schmalz. (Fred had coached Davis & Elkins

University and also moonlighted at my soccer school.) One evening, we went out to the famous Gilley's Club, known for its mechanical bulls. They advertised as the largest honky-tonk bar in the world, supplying patrons with a steady stream of country music. In we walked, and every cowboy turned his head to have a good look at the strange apparition that just breezed into their joint—the only black coach on the coaches' staff.

Standing with our backs to the bar, I whispered to Fred: "Things don't look good for me." Then up stands a man dressed in jeans, cowboy boots, and a short-sleeve shirt that strained to contain his biceps. He put a few quarters into a test-of-strength machine (a boxer's speed ball with a gauge attached to measure the force of the blow) pointed at me, and punched the bag with all his might. "Oh, Jesus," I muttered, as the proud puncher squinted at the readout. Fred was having a great time. A second cowboy does the same, and then a third. When they'd had their fun, I walked over and deposited my quarters. The place went quiet. I reared back and head-butted the bag full force. Man, you could hear a rat piss on cotton. Then the cowboys started laughing their asses off! They came over and bought us beer.

In my home state of Maryland, I also encountered the occasional racist gesture. In need of a driver's license renewal, I once drove out to the Department of Motor Vehicles (DMV) where I found the place shuttered. A man was standing at the door reading a notice when I pulled up. "What does it say?" I asked. "Why don't you get out and read it your goddamn self!" he snapped. I did, and followed the instructions to another location. On the way there, I saw the same guy, pulled over at the side of the road, fretting under the hood of his car. As I drove past, I thought I'd have some fun, so I made a U-turn and pulled up beside him.

"Sir, you seem to be having some trouble," I said. "Are you going to the DMV?" He looked at me warily, but climbed in. After I pulled off, there were a few moments of uncomfortable silence as he checked me out. "Are you the guy from the DMV?" he asked nervously. "Yup," I said, nodding slowly, with a beautiful smile in my heart. He asked why I'd stopped for him after he'd been so rude. I said I didn't know. I even dropped him back to his car that day. He took out his cheque book, but I stopped him, saying: "Pass it on."

You can deal with racial stereotyping in two ways: Bristle at the slightest provocation or laugh it off. One of the best laughs I ever had about racial expectations in the United States again involved the Department of Motor Vehicles.

I went to the DMV to license my car. Waiting for my name to be called, the customers were set a-twittering by a clerk who was clearly enjoying the line-up. He began with a list of names that included a Wild West outlaw, a cult leader, and a pop singer. "James, Jesse," he intoned drily. "Jones, Jim. Michael, George." Then came a string of presidents' names including Hoover and McKinley. People giggled. Finally, in a voice dripping with sarcasm, the clerk announced: "Lincoln, Abraham." As I picked my way to the counter, people guffawed. At the counter, the clerk gave me the once-over. "Abe?" he asked. I answered yes. He just shook his head. Wading back through the mostly white crowd, they patted me on the back: "Go on, Abe!"

Attending the National Coaches' Convention in the 1990s along with 35,000 others, I was struck by the underrepresentation of black coaches. Fewer than 10% of the coaches there were non-white. I knew from my decades in the U.S. that the discrimination against us was subtle but real. Too often, the best candidate has been overlooked because his skin is not white or he has a "funny" accent.

With the image of that convention fresh in my mind in 1996, I founded the Black Soccer Coaches Association to advocate for the hiring of non-white coaches. At first, some coaches argued that we should call it the Coloured Coaches Association, but the Jamaicans in particular backed me; they were adamant that we shouldn't be black apologists. We were proud of who we were.

One of the major achievements of the lobby group is that it's now mandatory to have a minimum of two black coaches as speakers at the annual coaches' convention, billed as the world's largest gathering of soccer coaches. There are still very few black coaches in the American pro-soccer league, but the university ranks are certainly more racially diverse than they were in my days at Howard. Some of this can be attributed to the work of the association. In 2000, the Black Soccer Coaches Association was struggling, so the National Soccer Coaches' Association of America took the organization under its umbrella as a committee.

I was lord of all I surveyed: Four hundred kids playing soccer simultaneously, under a coaching plan I'd devised. This was Prince William Soccer Incorporated (PWSI), a youth soccer club in Virginia.

I was its Director of Coaching. I'd created soccer stations spread over four fields—one for dribbling, another for heading, a third for passing—and every few minutes a horn blew, rotating the kids onto a new station. It was a thing of beauty.

The club's teams hadn't been doing well, in part because a few influential coaches controlled little fiefdoms and hogged all the good players for their own teams, which meant a few teams prospered while the majority suffered. I decided to start grading players from one to five, so players got to compete against others of similar skill. It also meant that the best coaches were paired with the best teams. Our teams started going to tournaments and winning. But of course, the coaches who lost powerful teams weren't happy. When I attempted to break up the club president's juggernaut, he threatened to take his team to another club.

I spent five years at PWSI in the 1990s, and took the club from 136th in the state to tenth. Part of what we did there was to de-emphasize the kind of over-coaching that can suck all the life from the game if you aren't careful. We coached, yes, but we also gave the kids time to kick a ball around. We set them up to play four-versus-four and gave them autonomy to pick captains and decide who played where.

When PWSI told me in 2000 that they'd "decided to go in a new direction," I took my leave without bitterness. With the help of a strong president by the name of Ed Foster-Simeon, I had helped turn the club around from a money-losing venture to a lucrative enterprise that was raking in coaching fees.

At Howard, I had written a letter I regretted. Now, I penned one I remain proud of today. I exhorted the club to greater heights and thanked everyone there. I said that working hard to overcome obstacles had made me a better coach. The letter remained on the PWSI website for several years. It's my reminder that when you leave a job, you should always go with dignity.

The Howard University Bisons soccer team never recaptured the championship-winning glory of the 1970s. In part, this is because the competition for players is more intense and the best players from Africa and the Caribbean are no longer coming exclusively to a relatively small school, albeit one with a proud history of "unashamed and unafraid blackness." The lucrative pro leagues of Europe have opened to these players, and so have the doors of many tertiary education institutions with vastly superior sporting facilities and more generous scholarships. The amount of homegrown American talent has also grown exponentially. Since soccer has never made real inroads into the African-American community, where football and basketball remain the dominant sports, Howard's soccer is unlikely to flourish again.

My successor as Howard coach, former assistant coach Keith Tucker, did get more Americans onto the squad. In 1988, he made it to an NCAA final with several African-Americans on the team.

Jamaican Mikey Davey, one of the keys to our 1974 season when we finished with a record of nineteen wins, no draws, no losses and the NCAA title, has mounted a campaign, almost forty years after the fact, to have a sign commemorating the championship re-installed on the Howard campus. The original sign read: "Howard University— Home of the 1974 National Collegiate Soccer Champions." The university seems to have forgotten the pride we brought, to the school, the city, and the black community.

Our championship plaque was chucked into storage under some stairs until the swim coach dug it out and displayed it in a trophy case that he had made himself.

Everywhere I've gone in the United States—Howard University, Gaithersburg, Baltimore—American football has been king. But I've lived to see soccer hustle its way to a position of some respectability. As a pro and a longtime coach, I like to believe that I've played some small role in helping the sport to the fore. At my induction into the Maryland Soccer Hall of Fame in 2012, as the emcee listed my accomplishments, a blurry image of the thousands of kids I'd coached flashed before me. One in particular reminded me of the game's transformative potential.

I was doing a clinic for the physically and mentally handicapped in Washington DC in the 1970s. The children were running around and having a blast; except for a stocky kid who stood on the field with his arms folded tightly across his chest in an X. The ball would hit him in his foot and he wouldn't move. He didn't even look down. His caregivers wanted to take him off the field, but I urged them to leave him on. The clinic lasted a few days, and finally, Mr. Impassive put toe to ball. It's a good thing I was born with the reflexes of a goalkeeper. That ball sizzled past my ear on its way to Baltimore. I can't take a lot of credit because I didn't do anything but leave the guy on the field, but it seemed to me yet another example of the wonders soccer can do.

The sport has carried me from the packed earth of my childhood abode to the barrack yard of the Trinidad and Tobago Regiment. It has launched me from the Pan Am Games podium to two NCAA titles. And it has lifted me from the bench of the Bays to several duels with the world's greatest player.

It has taken me above and beyond the crossbar.

Our championship-winning Howard team has reunited a couple times. At our 25th anniversary Amdemichael Selassie's wife approached me. Her husband, a fine goalkeeper, had been crucial in helping us to the 1974 final, but perhaps had reason to feel aggrieved at being left out for the championship match. Mrs. Selassie, a quiet lady, approached me and said: "Thank you for my husband."

I was perplexed, until she told me that when the couple faced problems, her husband often mentioned the ways in which we had overcome obstacles at Howard. It was the best tribute I could have hoped for.

Today I'm the assistant coach of Loyola University Maryland women's soccer team. Despite my bionic knees, these 72-year-old legs no longer afford me the liberty of demonstrating at full-speed; but the-hard drive up top has files upon files of experience to dispense. Once I had taught our number one goalkeeper when she should come off her line, she anchored the defence solidly, helping the school to the Metro Atlantic Athletic Conference title in 2012.

I still want to help young players in T&T to achieve their full potential. (Hopefully I can do it before the sand in my glass runs out.) And, I enjoy the role of mentor more than any other. To quote my protégé-cum-nemesis, Keith Look Loy: "The most important gift you can give to anyone is opportunity."

At Queen's Royal College in Trinidad, the prestige school that my entire family and a few close friends rallied to dress me for, a House has been named after me. It was the school's custom to divide the student population into four groups, or Houses, named after celebrated alumni. Eric Williams, the country's first prime minister, headed one; author, historian and Caribbean philosopher C.L.R. James another; Nobel Laureate in Literature V.S. Naipaul a third; and successful businessman Sir Lindsay Grant the fourth. When the school later decided to pair outstanding QRC athletes with great intellects, I was matched with C.L.R. James. My old friend, West Indies wicketkeeper Deryck Murray got Naipaul, Olympic medal-winning sprinter Wendell Mottley lined up beside Eric Williams, and world class cyclist Roger Gibbon teamed up with Grant.

One Friday afternoon in 2007, while working as technical director in Trinidad, I was strolling around the Queen's Park Savannah, where I had played many matches as a young man. Approaching the imposing red main building of my alma mater, I saw a little fellow dressed in the blue shirt-jack and long khaki pants of the school I had so longed to attend. He approached me quite unabashedly. "Ay, sir," he said. "I in your house. We in the blue house. We better than them other house. We does beat them up."

My goalkeeping book
goes to press.

Skipper Sedley Joseph regales
me with a tale at a ceremony
honouring Trinidad and
Tobago's football legends.

A FIFA symposium for
technical instructors in
Zurich, Switzerland.

Demonstrating a diving skill to
Todd Polhemus (R) in Alabama.

In Qatar at the closing
ceremony of a FIFA-
sponsored course.

Richard Braithwaite, former
FIFA/CONCACAF coaching
education director—the unsung
hero of T&T's 2006 World Cup.

President of Trinidad &
Tobago Noor Hassanali
inducts me into the National
Sporting Hall of Fame.

Two St. James boys—
Me (third from right)

Epilogue

"Coach"—the word still makes my head tingle with pride. Any title that designates a heightened level of respect and achievement would do the same, I expect: Doctor, Ambassador, Senator, Governor, Captain. But to me, Coach surpasses them all. It is he who helps people become their best.

A coach is a mentor, friend, disciplinarian, taskmaster, therapist, and confidant. He is brother, father, and educator. For many of those who play sports, Coach is someone who shapes and influences their lives, for better OR for worse. It is an awesome responsibility, and I have cherished it from the moment I was first chosen to lead.

How did I find myself on such a path? I can only look to those who affected my life with selfless compassion and commitment of their time. It was my mentors who led me here, however unwitting that may have been.

Here is what I believe: To help others, you must also learn to recognize and accept help when it is needed.

Along with saying "sorry," we men find asking for help a most difficult thing to do. But asking for help increases one's capacity to give help when the moment arises. The African philosophy of *ubuntu* says that my humanity rests on my ability to recognize the humanity of others. Coaches, like others who help people fulfill their full potentials, do so simply because they see themselves. I was once that little boy, juggling a ball on his boot.

Times have changed. As I reflect upon my experiences, I sometimes wonder what will become of Coach in this culture of headphone-wearing isolation.

I know there are good young coaches out there; I helped produce some of them. And I'm sure they will find a way to reach the next generation of players. Their reward will be what my reward has always been. Just call me Coach.

Acknowledgements

This book has taken such a long time to write. There are so many people to thank and acknowledge, not only for their encouragement, but also for their friendship and guidance. This is such a wonderful opportunity for me to reach out to some of the important people in my life; especially those who have played some part in this biography. If you are not mentioned, and think you should be, let me know. I always like to be reminded of who my friends are.

Firstly I want to thank Valentino Singh and Robert Clarke for the encouragement they provided in getting the manuscript off the ground. Those two years of Sunday morning interviews came as a treat, as I relived every aspect of my life. Unfortunately, I left Trinidad to return to the United States at the end of my football administration contract, but I hit the jackpot and my good fortune continued. The Good Lord guided me, via Ian Bain, to a resourceful, energetic writer named Robert Clarke who undertook the task of bringing the book to fruition. My heart goes out to these two excellent writers for making my life's journey blossom before my very eyes.

I also feel grateful to the members of my Think Tank—Sheldon Phillips, Victor Gamaldo, Dr. Trevor Leiba, Dr. Peter Keiller and Ian Bain—for their enthusiasm and support from the very beginning. They kept me going through several major hiccups, and have been a joy to work with. They have been very forthright and meticulous, keeping me alert to the fact that we all want this book to enlighten, entertain and motivate.

I want to thank my agent, Rock Newman—one of the most dynamic and informative talk show personalities in Washington, D.C. He got involved when the manuscript was finished, but the ethos he brought to the whole process burned so bright that everyone involved in this project began to see and feel the real significance of the book.

I wish to extend my deepest gratitude to Pauline Philip for editing the manuscript on short notice. This kind gesture came at a time when the coffers were bare and the need for quality editing was critical.

Brian Lewis, the President of the Trinidad and Tobago Olympic Committee deserves more than just a mention here; he is the one who came up with the title of my biography: *Above and Beyond the Crossbar.* I am truly grateful for your thoughtfulness and creativity in selecting such an appropriate title.

Ah! My family. I love you so much for what you have provided me. My life's foundation was heavily influenced by you and I wish to thank you all for who I am today.

My grandfather, James "Dada" Cumberbatch, came from Barbados at the age of seventeen. He contributed to my competence in reading, even at a very young age. When his eyesight was failing, he was unable to read the newspapers. I read them to him daily and was handsomely compensated with a penny each time.

I want to express my sincere gratitude for the way my mother raised us. She instilled in us all the virtues we needed to be well-rounded individuals. She provided all the love and attention and shared our passion for sport. My mom was indeed a champion!

My Dad was one of the most important people in my life. He came to visit us twice a week and I saw him on a regular basis at his various job sites. He instilled in me a sense of responsibility and pride, not only in completing tasks, but in doing them as well as possible. I admired his work ethic and creativity in every job entrusted to him. I can certainly say that I feared, respected and loved him simultaneously. As a father, I know that only successful parents inspire that rare combination of emotions in the right proportions.

I am very fortunate to have grown up with my siblings around me. I will always be grateful for the love, compassion, thoughtfulness and protection that my eldest sister Alicia provided me in the early stages of my life. While Mom was away working two or three jobs, Babsie (as we so affectionately called her) took on the role of sister/mom. All I can say is that she took her job very seriously!

I wish to thank Wilbert. He was my oldest brother living at home. The "Bull" was everything I could ever dream of in a big brother. He taught me everything—the good, the bad, and the ugly. All the nice, gory things a little boy needs to know. A fierce protector of his siblings, you could expect a severe pummeling from "D Bull" if you touched his little brother. This protective attitude continued well into adulthood.

Georgie, my paternal brother, was my mentor! During my tempestuous years as Technical Director for the Trinidad & Tobago Football Federation, he was always there for me, offering his usual kind words and solutions to the myriad problems I faced. A fierce competitor, Georgie taught me how to be EX-tremely combative during a game, to leave all battles on the field of play, and to resume my life, with friends and even my brother, afterward. Winner of the Hummingbird Medal, Georgie served his community as seriously as he lived his life. He was indeed my role model and I thank him up to this day for influencing my life in such a positive way.

My younger siblings . . .

Marilyn ("Cookie" as I so lovingly call her) was totally spoilt. Our grandfather and aunts who lived in the same compound showered her with love. As we grew older, Cookie became my consummate playmate, laughing at all my silly jokes and singing the popular songs. As I gained popularity as a sports personality, Cookie became my most ardent supporter. Indeed, having a baby sister to play with and look after is truly a wonderful opportunity.

My two younger paternal brothers, Winston and Euan, were a lot of fun growing up. They came into my life in a big way when Wilbert went off to work on a boat. At their home at Ana Street, Woodbrook, we played our hearts out: cricket, soccer, and any other sport or game you could think of. Being a few years older, I was measurably stronger, and more competent and skilful at every sport we played. I enjoyed winning at everything (especially cricket) until, over a period of two to three years, I found that I no longer had a great advantage. Little did I know that Winston was being coached at Paragon Club. I now had to work exceedingly hard to beat them in any sport. I am truly grateful for the opportunity to hone my skills with the boys, especially in my formative years. Winston went on to play at left-back for the Trinidad & Tobago Regiment football team and later on developed one of the most lethal long throws in the history of football. He represented the national team on several occasions. I want to recognize, acknowledge and applaud them both for contributing to the development of my athletic career.

Just the mention of my uncles, aunts and cousins brings back so much joy and laughter. In the summer holidays, Wilbert and I spent quality time (sometimes days) at our Uncle Earnest's place in Boissiere Village, Maraval, and Uncle Sonny's farm in La Puerta, Diego Martin.

Uncle Earnest and Aunt Sible . . .
They were staunch Jehovah's Witnesses who had seven children. The oldest was Lisney, very stoic and a bit hoity-toity; then Clara, a toned-down Lisney; Sam, a cool and quiet guy; and Clyde, a real cool cat who loved every sport but was seriously challenged in ALL. Then there were the middle-order guys, around my age: Daniel, strangely quiet and always building something; Phyllis, the rebel; Richard, happy-go-lucky and always laughing his head off at my jokes; and the baby of the family, David.

Uncle Sonny and Aunt Levinia . . .
On the farm there were seven children. Roy was much older and an extremely good sportsman, and May was quiet and lovable. Then there were folks closer to my age: Janice, very impassive and a bit superior, but playful; Wilton, very good at sports; Urla, a year younger and fun-loving; Linda, a bit younger than me with a great personality; and the youngest, Everald, who always had a very sad countenance but was playful when coaxed.

What amazed me most was how everyone loved each other. These folks were always so happy to see Wilbert and me. Searching for fruits in the forest and playing games of every description are pastimes that have stayed in my heart. I have taken the time to mention all these folks because they were a very important part of my world.

My in-laws . . .

I am eternally grateful for the friendship and camaraderie I have shared with all my in-laws: Victor and Eula Gamaldo, Janet and Emerick Brown, Trevor and Siobhan D'Andrade, Grace Phillips, Helena Phillips, Julia Phillips, Melodie Phillips, Gloria Cumberbatch, Poo Ying Phillips, Carl Joyeau, Carl Alfonso, and the others who I have omitted but certainly not forgotten.

I am so very proud of my four sons: Sheldon, Sean, Gregory and Derek. They have grown up so fast. Each has earned the title of "Protector." In my book, there is no higher distinction. They love, honour, respect and protect their families with all their hearts.

Thank you so much Sheldon for your tremendous support with all my endeavours over the years. Good luck with your new job as General Secretary of the Trinidad and Tobago Football Association. Your degree in Law coupled with your experience working with the FIFA World Cup Committee and the Olympics in Atlanta will serve you in good stead.

Sean, you have blessed me with three beautiful grandchildren— Zara (19), Marco (17), and Tyler-Max (7). I am very proud of them. Good luck with your coaching career, as you add the responsibility of assistant coach of Notre Dame women's soccer program to your two girls' teams. Your vast experience as a professional soccer player will help you to lead your charges to success. Good luck with you new business ventures: "One to Turn To" and "The Art Of Soccer."

Gregory, you have brought so much to my life: Love, thrills and excitement. Some of it I prefer not to remember. Watching you battle on that hospital bed for over a month after your accident was truly an ordeal, which only brought the family closer. Finally, I do admire your courage and determination to go against-the-grain in so many decisions. You always seem to be marching to your own drum, and that shows courage. Indeed, courage is the first of human qualities because it is the quality that guarantees all others.

And last, but by no means least, Derek. Your time in Germany and Ireland as a professional soccer player and your short stint with the Trinidad & Tobago World Cup Team (until you were sidelined by injury) led you to your job as strength and conditioning coach of the women's soccer program at Loyola University Maryland. I love talking soccer with you while driving to work. I know you're living out your dream of entrepreneurship as owner of "Inside Out Performance." I truly love and appreciate my grandchildren—Jah (14), Joy (4), and Kenzie (8 weeks). All my 'grands' are precious. The girls smother me in hugs and kisses, and I get to romp and play soccer with the boys. What more could I ask for?

To all my dear friends—those who are with us today and others who have moved on to a better place—thank you for your friendship over the years. Thank you Anthony Campbell and Deryck Murray for your long and dear friendships, and for paving the way for me to get into QRC. My deepest appreciation goes out to Anthony Ferguson and Anton LaFond for their long years of encouragement to return to Trinidad & Tobago football. Thanks to Raymond Tim Kee for his moral support in difficult times during my tenure as technical director. Rudy Thomas and Mohammed Isa, how can I forget those long hours we spent together, working on the TTFF development program? Ken Butcher, your tremendous support through the Sports Company was truly a blessing; I owe you and your dear wife Pat so much for what you did in the early stages of my tenure in Trinidad. The times I spent with you both were enjoyable, enlightening and inspirational. Bishop Brown, your prayers and timely advice were always appreciated; I will always remember you, my friend. I will always remember the moral and professional support of Myron Garnes, Earl McEachron, John Taylor, Andy Zvara, Sook Lee, Ruthvyn Charles, Dr. Iva Gloudon, Garnett Albert, Peta Bain, Mary Siu Butt, and George Jefferson. Andre Baptiste, "D Fearless one," I cannot begin to tell you how much I appreciate your support in the media. As well as providing me with the opportunity to practice a bit of live game commentary, you always protected me from meanness. Joel Villafana, Flex Mohammed, George Jefferson and Fazeer Mohammed, as members of the media you always respected and appreciated my efforts; especially when the going was rough.

I want to extend my sincerest gratitude and appreciation to my dear colleagues at Howard University for providing me with the opportunity, not only to establish myself as a premier college level coach, but to further my education and earn my Bachelor's and Master's degrees in Physical Education.

I would like to extend my sincerest gratitude to all my fellow coaches and colleagues of the Trinidad and Tobago Football Association, the Sports Company of Trinidad & Tobago, the National Soccer Coaches Association of America, the United States Soccer Federation, and the Virginia & Maryland Youth Soccer Association. Special thanks to the Old Boys Association of Maryland; the Black Soccer Coaches Association; all the players staff, colleagues, parents and friends of the Soccer Association of Columbia and Prince William Soccer Inc. My association with you folks over the years has indeed been a blessing and I truly love you all so very much for helping me enjoy over forty years of life in the United States. You will always be remembered for your loving kindness and support in good times and bad.

Finally, I must acknowledge my dear wife Linda. Beautiful, funny, sensual, talented, and above all the best wife a man could ever dream of. She has played a major role in every one of my accomplishments. Her love and devotion to me, our children and grandchildren is unsurpassable. She has given me four of the best sons a father could dream of having.

I owe it all to my wife, Linda Felicia.

I wish to share this book with all my teammates and the players I coached through the years.

- **Spatax F.C.** – *Kirt Williams, Ainsley Julal, Courtney Julal, Renald Julal, Kelvin Williams, Joe Hinds, Kenrick Wilson, Mosely Jack, Wilfred Perry, Ralph Hall, Clyde Corintine, Winston Evelyn, Lance Farrell, Rudy Roberts.*

- **Wanderers** – *Selwyn St. Louis, Benito Sambrano, Carl Russell, Eve Russell, Noel James, Winston Phillips, Luc-oo.*

- **Starlets** – *Anthony Campbell, Frankie Williams, Pops Blanchefield.*

- **Providence**—*Jazzy Pantin, Rugged Tom, Arthur Belgrave, Dennis Thomas, Skinner, Desmond Blackman, Carl Blackman, Joe Hinds, Lester Herbert.*

- **Queen's Royal College (QRC)** – *Johnny Perreira, Ian Jones, Winty Samuel, Kenny Nasib, Billy Samuel, Deryck Murray, Bunny Bessor, Hubert Gamaldo, Victor Gamaldo, McGregor Hinkson, Anthony Campbell, Holly Carrington, Ray Raymond, Rawle Boland, Dwight Day, Chris Rudder.*

- **Woolsey Touring XI**—*Bob Cheewah, Drayton, Boysie Rampersad, Tolai, Carlton Franco, Alvin Corneal, Clive Niles, Robbie Greenidge, Percy Pierre.*

- **Bertie Thompson Touring XI** – *Ken Henry, Tyrone De La Bastide, Hugh Mulzack, Carlton Francis, Patrick Raymond, Anthony Skerrett, Dennis Blackman, Dennis Thomas, Ian Drayton, Carlton Franco.*

- **Maple** – *Andy Aleong, Alvin Corneal, Sedley Joseph, Sacky Hoford, Eddy Aleong, Renwick Metiveau, Clevy Caracciolo, David McDeggan, Bing Licorich, Conrad Braithwaite, Ri, Hugo Along, Tyrone De La Bastide, David Lamy, Matthew Nunes, Ron Woods, Dick Rodriguez, Gaga Garcia, Kush Holder.*

- **Trinidad & Tobago Regiment** – *Keith Richards, Steve Henry, Kelvin Berassa, Clive Niles, Wilfred Lewis, Victor Gamaldo, Euan Phillips, Cax Paul, Johnny Francois, Sharky Henry, Benito Sambrano, Tony Inniss, Charlie Spooner, Philbert Prince,*

Winston Phillips, Lance Farrell, Miley Yorke, Godfrey Achille, Lenny Gill, Gerry Brown, Secky Stewart, Tim Lambkin, Dennis Thomas, Joe Simon, Leslie Wright.

- **Baltimore Bays** – *Gordon Jago—coach, Gary Powell—assistant coach* **(United States)** *Lief Klasson* **(Sweden)** *Gaucho Tejada, Calixto Mendes, Juan Santistaban, Lopez, Carmelo Cedrún* **(Spain)** *Terry Adlington, Dennis Viollet, Wilf Tranter, Mike Davies* **(England)** *Art Welch, Asher Welch, Winston Earle* **(Jamaica)** *Uriel DeVega, Zamaria* **(Brazil)** *Orlando Rysenburg* **(Suriname)** *Yaw Kam Kam* **(Ghana)** *Rusty Kindratew, Joey Speca* **(United States)** *Guy St. Ville* **(Haiti)** *David Primo* **(Israel).**

- **Baltimore Comets**—*Hank Kazmierski, Alan Mayer, Billy Loehr, Paul Scurti, Geoff Butler,*

- *Dennis Wit, John Gibbon* **(USA)** *Paul Scurti, Alvin Henderson, Keith Aqui, Victor Gamaldo* **(Trinidad & Tobago)** *Zlato Tripkovic, Peter Sylvester, Ken Hill, Frank Largo.*

- **Washington Darts** – *Bertram Grell, Gerry Brown, LeRoy Deleon, Selris Figaro, Winston Alexis, Warren Archibald, Everald Cummings, Victor Gamaldo* **(Trinidad)** *Aldo Zito* **(Brazil)** *Raymond Crispin, Roland Crispin* **(Haiti)** *John Kerr, Billy Fraser, Frank Donlevy, Danny Payton* **(Scotland)** *Guy Fraiture* **(Belgium)** *Miguel Diego* **(Spain)** *Willie Evans, Joseph Gyau* **(Ghana)** *John Hanson* **(Canada)** *Carl Minor* **(Australia)** *Romulo Cortez* **(Bolivia)** *Victorio Casa* **(Argentina)** *Nick Papadakis, Alex Papadakis* **(Greece)** *John Muir* **(England).**

- **Howard University** – *Michael Billy Jones, William Aboke-Cole* **(Sierra Leone)** *Donnie Simmons, Stan Smith, Orlando Simmons, Keith Tucker, Edmund Talbot, Gerard Basden* **(Bermuda)** *Keith Aqui, Alvin Henderson, Edward Holder, Desmond Alfred, Steve Waldron, Winston Yallery-Arthur, Ian Bain, Keith Look Loy, Neil Williams, Tony Martin, Trevor Leiba, Trevor Mitchell, Neil Cuthbert, Gerard Johnson, Peter De Coteau, Roger Hicks, Ernest Skinner – manager* **(Trinidad & Tobago)** *Olosegun Onadeku, Charlie Pyne, Frank Oshin, Tunde Balogun, Yomi Bamiro, Kenneth Ilodigwe, Dominic Ezeani,*

*Miyiwa Sanya, Sunday Izevbigie, Shola Popola, Omo Esemuede, Ephraim Inameti, Edmund Ezurike, Sylvanus Oriakhi, Edmund Olumekor, Olawunmi Isegen, Tony Amayo (**Nigeria**) Zewdu Haptamarium, Salah Yousif – scout (**Ethiopia**) Jacques Ladouceur (**Haiti**) Terrence Whall, Sandy (**Guyana**) Michael Tomlinson, Keith Tulloch, Lincoln Peddie, Bertram Beckett, Gilbert McPherson, Conrad Seymour, Carlton Briscoe, Michael McPherson, David Johnson, Gerald Duggan, Ian Gage, Donnie Street, Bancroft Gordon, Richard Davy, Errol Gillette, Mike Anderson, Lloyd Anderson, Mikey Davey, Kenneth Davy, Paul Pringle, Mario Mc Lennan, Colin McLean, Everton Harrison (**Jamaica**) Andy Terrell, William Peterson, Kenneth Pollard, Carl Bonner, Henry Gillem, Trey Black, Terry Fontanelle, Robert Dawson, James Sansom, Frank Craford, Mark McClellan, Ted Chambers – assistant coach, Milton Miles—trainer (**USA**) Mori Diane (**Guinea**) Amdemichael Selassie (**Eritrea**) Samuel Tetteh, Sam Acqua (**Ghana**).*

- **Gaithersburg High School** – *Erik Kasari, Tita Kasari, Artheu Singh, Mark Baba, Matt Polster, David Barnes, Julian Etches, Mike Nelson, Eric Nelson, Mark Bak, Eric Cismanec, Ian Gerdes, Mark Kurup, Paul Wenninger, Scott Oh.*

- **Maryland Bays** – *Steve Powers, Nick Broujis, Paul Emorodi, John Karpovich, Eric Hawkes, John Abe, Stan Lambros, Veron Skinner, Paul Rutenis, Chris Reif, Darryl Dee, Philip Gyau, Joe Barger, Amir Parsa, Darius Bujak, Rich Ryerson, Rob Ryerson, Elvis Comrie, Scott Cook, Kurt Dashbac, Drago Dumbovich, Stan Koziol, Sam Mangione, Jeff Nattans, David Nakhid, Junior Nichols, Kevin Sloan.*

- **Virginia Commonwealth University (VCU)**—*Mark Huff, Chris Thomas, Matt Thomas, Anil Roberts, Jason Gordon, Bart Polster, Kevin Whitlock, Steve Amedio, Anthony Briatico, Frank Belen, Eric Butler, Justin Powers, Sean Moriaty, Marty Pritchett, Kwaku Adu-Gyamfi, Omar Castillo, Jasen Elsmore, Chris Gavilan, Brian Kirchdorfer, Neil Mason, Romano Paul, Jon DeLong, Jeff Oberg, Eric Dade, Wayne Pratt, Kevin Moze, William Wright, Frank Roxenius, Wayne Goring, Michael Hitchcock, Frank Owusu, Peter Roberts, Anthony Sherwood,*

Leroi Wilson, Peter McNally, Chris Gavilan, Jay Sullivan, Chris Dvorac, Chris Barnard, Vladislav Bez borodov, Jason Helmlinger, Cory Osterbingd, Mervyn Wright, Keith Englehardt, Michael Gill, Jonathan Morris, Cory Smith, Antonio Frederich, Fredrik Wickstrom, Antonio Vaughn, Michael Wright, Greg Wise, Jason Shepard.